"Finding and following God's will is one of the greatest spiritual challenges we grapple with—in times of crisis, certainly, and also in daily living. Jane Kise's book is both practical and inspirational, with scriptural tools and compelling real-life stories of people who have learned to discern and accept God's will. What a good way to help readers make the most of their own journeys of spiritual discovery!"

—**Amy Wong,** managing editor, *Guideposts*

"Jane Kise creates a valuable lesson for Christians of all ages in Finding and Following God's Will. *Using Bible stories, as well as reflections from her own life and the lives of friends, Jane shares her insight and hope. This is sure to bless and encourage your heart."*

—**Tracie Peterson,** award-winning, bestselling author, HEIRS OF MONTANA series

JANE A.G. KISE is the coauthor of more than a dozen books, including *LifeKeys: Discover Who You Are, Did You Get What You Prayed For?,* and *Find Your Fit.* In addition to school staff development consulting she teaches seminars on prayer, spirituality, and finding meaning and purpose in life. Jane has an MBA in finance and a doctorate in eductional leadership. She and her family live in Minneapolis, Minnesota.

*To find out more about Jane Kise's books*
*visit the Web site: www.janekise.com.*

## Bethany House Books by Jane A.G. Kise

Finding and Following God's Will
Find Your Fit
LifeDirections
LifeKeys: Discover Who You Are

# Finding and Following God's Will

## Jane A.G. Kise

BETHANYHOUSE
Minneapolis, Minnesota

**Library of Congress Cataloging-in-Publication Data**

Kise, Jane A. G.
    Finding and following God's will / by Jane A.G. Kise.
        p.   cm.
    Summary: "How, when, and why does God talk to people today? In tackling these questions, this book helps readers discern God's will for their lives"—Provided by the publisher.
    ISBN 0-7642-0026-7 (pbk.)
    1. Discernment (Christian theology)   2. God—Will.   I. Title.
    BV4509.5.K489      2005
    248.4—dc22                                                    2004027874

For Dan
*May you continue to*
*find and follow God's pathways for you!*

# Contents

# God's Will . . . A Map or a Process?

Lake Burntside. Virgin pines line the rocky outcroppings of its shores, their rugged appearance softened by an occasional sandy beach. Loons cry back and forth every hour of the day, their laughter cackling across the water as they take flight. For those who listen carefully, at night the thin howl of a wolf might rise toward the pitch-black heavens where stars shine undimmed by city lights.

Lake Burntside is our home away from home—my husband, Brian, and I even honeymooned there. The lake is huge, 74 miles of shoreline and at least 125 islands. Nestled in at the edge of the Boundary Waters Canoe Area Wilderness (BWCAW), the north arm of the lake houses a few secluded cabins, a YMCA camp for teens, and one for families. We've served as volunteer staff for several years at the family camp, leading voyager canoe paddles, adult blueberry expeditions through national forest trails, and canoe trips through winding rivers. We're experienced canoeists, breezing through portages in one trip. Brian, who grew up on a lake, often skippers the camp's pontoon boat.

A couple of years ago at the family camp, Brian and I arranged activities for a young woman with special needs. Because she couldn't canoe, we chose a cloudy but dry morning to offer her a pontoon boat tour of the lake.

Boats and water are always dangerous, so we planned for safety. We took her mother and another able-bodied couple along just in case.

We added extra life jackets for good measure.

We tucked water bottles, rain gear, sunscreen, and bug spray into a day pack.

Brian checked the gas cans.

We didn't grab a map because we only planned to head down the main channel, circle the first couple of islands, and head back.

But the sun peeked out as we motored onto the main lake, so our expedition voted to go a bit farther. Our guests laughed as loons dived, then popped up closer to us.

A shadow passed over the boat. I caught Brian's eye and pointed to a fast-moving bank of dark clouds rolling in from the west.

"I think that concludes our tour," Brian quipped as he swung the wheel and headed the boat back north. Within minutes, huge drops of rain splattered the water. I helped our guests into rain gear, then walked over to sit next to Brian. He was frowning, peering around at the shoreline.

"Where's the channel?" I asked.

"It's over there . . . I think. I'm trying to remember how many islands we circled."

And we hadn't brought a map. Like a couple of greenhorns instead of the expert guides we considered ourselves. A solid wall of rain raced in behind us. Brian pulled closer to shore. The young disabled woman with us could barely walk, so I took note of a lone private dock that could be temporary refuge if we heard thunder. *What were we thinking, not bringing a map?* I chastised myself.

While not taking a map was stupid (navigating among the islands is tricky even when you have one along), we didn't panic. We put our heads together with the other couple and picked out the most likely bearings for the channel among the islands and coves ahead. A few turns later, we spotted the narrows. Within fifteen minutes, we pulled in at the camp dock, somewhat soaked but safe.

———

Even without a map, we had tools for guidance: Brian's boating experience, our collective wisdom about the shoreline and storm safety, and knowledge of the safe havens at hand. It was enough to get us home.

Lakes in the wilderness aren't the only places we feel lost in life. Job changes, relationships, illnesses, problems with finances, or that old car that simply won't start, leave us wondering whether we made a wrong turn onto a dead-end path or even whether we're totally lost.

The feeling can be paralyzing. You'd do anything for a map of the future with clear direction. *Tell me what to do,* you might pray. And if an answer doesn't come, you may start wondering if God has abandoned you. *God, you guided the Israelites through the wilderness, you showed Paul where to go, you gave Moses a burning bush, Gideon the fleeces . . . why can't I have a pillar of fire to show the way, too?*

Ponder, though, how the Israelites reacted to being guided night and day.

They grumbled about the food.

They complained when water supplies ran short.

They criticized their leaders and even threatened to stone Moses.

They turned their backs on God completely, melting their jewelry into a tangible god they could worship instead of the invisible yet loving God who brought them out of Egypt.

Do you still want a map?

Somehow, human nature gets twisted when we don't have to think for ourselves. In these pages, you'll find stories of people, both biblical and modern, who desperately sought God's guidance. Occasionally the answers came as clear as pillars of fire. More often, though, as in our pontoon boat adventure, the answers came in other ways.

God doesn't guide us just through signs and wonders, but through three other systems as well:

*The Bible.* Without a map, Brian and I read the shoreline, looking for dips in the trees, recognizable rocks, and certain cabins to find our way. There was plenty of information already around us to get us home. Similarly, the Bible's sixty-six books contain timeless truths for guiding our lives. Sometimes all the guidance we need is already there for us to read.

*Our own gifts.* Brian knew boats, how to steer in a storm, how to handle the waves. He could confidently offer a pontoon tour. The gifts and talents we have come from God and are part of how God gives us direction.

*Circumstances.* We didn't need a map to read the clouds and head for safety. Nor would the map have helped us find shelter as much as our own perusal of the available rocks and dock. Circumstances—"open doors and closed doors"—are a part of how God guides us. But note that in the absence of lightning, we kept moving despite the "open door" of a safe dock. Sometimes we rush for an open door, only to find it wasn't a sign from God at all.

God gives us four guidance systems then, not just direct "burning bush, writing on the wall, angel visit" direction. The other three seem to help us draw closer to our Creator who loves us no matter how far we stray.

As you read these pages, take inventory of your agility with all four systems. Can you use them all? It is my prayer that even in the midst of a storm, with no map, you'll be able to navigate safely back to where God wants you to be.

August 2004
Camp du Nord, Lake Burntside

# Suggestions for Allowing *Finding and Following God's Will* to Speak to You

Discovering God's will is a lifelong journey; when you're on a journey, a straight line isn't always the most pleasant route between where you are and your destination. Sometimes it's the detours, the rest stops, the refreshing pauses at scenic overlooks, the days spent at museums full of treasures, or hills worth the climb that are the purpose of your trip.

While you can certainly read *Finding and Following God's Will* from start to finish, you can also personalize your journey depending on your questions and struggles in discovering what God wants you to do. Any path through its pages is filled with possibilities for new discoveries and insights. Consider the following suggestions for making your journey as meaningful as possible.

*Start with your heart.* You might feel most comfortable beginning with the first chapter. That's fine. Consider, though, perusing the table of contents; the chapter titles form a list of common questions people have about discovering God's will for their lives. Which question most intrigues you, seems most outlandish, or has kept you awake at night as uncertainties and concerns swirl through your thoughts? Start with that chapter.

*Ponder with pen and paper.* Each chapter features a retelling of a biblical story and three modern-day tales from people who set out to discover what God wanted them to do. As you read, jot down questions you'd like to ask the writer, experiences in your own life that are similar, and points you'd like to argue. You could either dedicate a notebook to this or write in the book's margins.

*Rest and reflect.* After each chapter, work through the Bible study questions that start on page 199. The questions are designed to enhance understanding, lend scriptural support, and allow for discussion of the concepts and stories presented in the chapter. Again, consider recording your questions, answers, and insights in a notebook.

*Pause for prayer.* After finishing the Bible study, look back through the questions the chapter raised in your mind. Have any of them been answered for you? Do you have more to add to your list? Consider praying over them to see what else God might have to say to you. Try praying in any of the following ways:

- Silently or aloud, ask each question, then pause to hear what God might tell you.
- Consider writing letters to God. Ask your questions, adding details from events in your own life or others'. Be honest about your struggles and frustrations as you write, just as the writers of the Psalms were.
- Copy a few of the phrases or Bible verses from the chapter or Bible study that were particularly meaningful for you or that raised specific questions. Place them in a spot where you can use them for prayer—on your bathroom mirror, above the kitchen sink, in your day planner, on the dashboard—whenever you have a moment of quiet in your day.
- Make your questions into a list as part of a prayer journal. Do some of your questions require more study? Could discussions with other people provide new insights? Do you need to look for concrete places where God is acting to understand how God would have you proceed? Refer back to your journal frequently and record progress you make in answering your questions.

*Join others for the journey.* The Bible study questions provide direction for group discussion. Before you begin, have everyone complete the chart on the following page and compare results. I've found that acknowledging the variety of opinions and comfort levels with the way God leads us allows for honesty and open discussion. It may also help remind everyone that discovering God's will is a mystery. Theologians have debated for years how to listen for God with certainty; I don't pretend to have all the answers but hope that the stories in these pages will help you learn from others who are doing their best to find God's best for their lives.

## Before You Begin . . .

"The place God calls you to is the place where your deep gladness and the world's deep hunger meet." Frederick Buechner, *Wishful Thinking*

Mark where you think you fall on the following continuums. There aren't any right or wrong answers, but this may help you gauge your reactions to *Finding and Following God's Will* and discern what next steps you might wish to take in discovering the gift of God's guidance.

### What role does God play in our lives?

God has no specific
plans for our lives

???

God will always
perfectly, obviously show
us what we should do

### How comfortable are you with using the following forms of guidance?

#### Scripture

I'm uncomfortable
using the Bible
for guidance

???

I know how to
use the Bible

#### Our unique gifts and talents

I'm not sure of
my gifts and talents

???

I understand how
God guides me
through my special design

#### Direct leadings

God no longer
speaks directly to us

???

God has spoken
directly to me through dreams,
angels, images, visions, etc.

#### Our circumstances

Our circumstances
do not tell us what
God wants us to do

???

God speaks to me
through circumstances

# 1

# Why Is It So Hard to Discover God's Will?

Key: The first step in finding God's will is giving our lives to God.

*Ten Jewish men. That was the minimum number needed to establish a synagogue. In a synagogue, men and women sat apart. Men led the reading and explanations of the sacred texts and the prayers. Only men could question the rabbis. Philippi, a Roman colony in northern Greece, fell short of ten Jewish men. No synagogue, no gathering place for worship and study of the law.*

*In towns without a synagogue, though, a custom arose. Each Sabbath, Jews gathered by a river outside of town to pray. Perhaps rivers reminded them of the everlasting love of God. Perhaps rivers brought to mind Ezekiel's vision of a new temple from which a river flowed, nourishing all the land. Or perhaps they thought of their ancestors in exile who sang, "By the waters of Babylon we sat down and wept when we remembered Zion."[1] Whatever the root of the custom, the apostle Paul knew that the river was the most likely place to find worshippers of Yahweh on a Sabbath morning.*

———

Lydia and her servants hurried past the city gates, away from the vendors' cries and the push of the crowds in the marketplace. The Sabbath in Philippi was no different than any other day. *Remember the Sabbath day and keep it holy . . .* She knew the law. Here, though, Yahweh seemed crowded out, even more so than in her hometown of Thyatira. This Roman town had a sanctuary to the Egyptian god Isis, one for Serapis, another for Dionysus, and statues of Caesar, but no synagogue.

At home, a synagogue surrounded them for worship even if the insignificant building was a poor substitute for Jerusalem's temple. *Jerusalem.* Some of her merchant friends had traveled there, returning with descriptions of the temple towers gleaming in the sun. Maybe she would glimpse its golden roofs before she died. Maybe next year she'd take the purple dye she sold, coveted for silken garments and the fringes of prayer shawls, to the City of David herself.

Her ears caught the gentle gurgle of the Gangas River. She quickened her step, catching her first glimpse of the sunlight playing across the rippling waters. Surely Yahweh smiled as they gathered here each week. She glanced at the servant women who accompanied her. They, too, seemed eager to honor the Sabbath day.

A small group had already spread their cloaks over the rough grasses that edged the stream, a few women and four men whom she didn't recognize. She shook out the cloak she'd carried over her arm, then sat down.

One of the men began reciting, "Hear O Israel, the Lord our God, the Lord is one . . ." The familiar prayers rose from the group. Lydia quickly perused the strangers, then looked down again. Foreigners, from the look of them. And they'd been traveling quite a while, too, judging by the worn look of their tunics. Her expert eyes detected the good quality of the cloth they were made from. Not beggars, certainly, but not well-to-do merchants like herself, either. What brought them to Philippi?

The same stranger spoke again. His companions leaned back and relaxed, as if they were used to listening to him. "My name is Paul, a Pharisee, of the house of Benjamin, a keeper of the law. Yet God has only begun to work within me."

Lydia looked up, startled. She'd never heard a Pharisee admit to being less than perfect.

He continued, "Jews everywhere await the Messiah to rescue us from Roman rule and restore the kingdom of Israel. But hear the words of Isaiah, 'He was crushed for our iniquities . . . by his wounds we are healed.'[2] Does that sound like the savior the Zealots are watching for? No, our Messiah has already come, and we didn't recognize him!"

Paul continued, interweaving Scripture and the life of a man called

Jesus. The sounds of the river, the rustle of the cooling breeze through the tree leaves, the dove in the tree, all faded away as her whole being pondered Paul's words. *Can this be true?* Lydia thought, glancing at the surprised faces of the women around her.

As Paul finished, he and the other men started softly singing a hymn,

> . . . but made himself nothing,
> taking the very nature of a servant
> . . . that at the name of Jesus every knee should bow,
> in heaven and on earth and under the earth,
> and every tongue confess that Jesus Christ is Lord,
> to the glory of God the Father.[3]

*Messiah as servant, not conqueror, showing us how to be obedient,* Lydia pondered. Somehow, it seemed right. The power of the stranger's message must have come from God! Something in their eyes, their bearing, kept Lydia from worries about whether they were just another band of false prophets.

Lydia joined in as the men repeated the hymn. Her heart sang along with her voice. As their singing faded with the last words, Paul looked at each face in the little circle of worshippers. He spoke again, his plea seeming to hang in the air, "Believe in him and you shall be saved." Paul's glance caught her eye. He nodded and smiled. She heard her voice asking, "Can we be baptized now?" She looked at her servants, who nodded their assent.

———

*Lydia and her household were the first Europeans baptized into the Christian faith, right there at the river where the Jews of Philippi gathered to worship and pray. Then she invited Paul and his companions to stay with her.*

*Lydia had no hesitation because she was already looking for God, making space in her life for prayer and worship, gathering with other women who also sought to do God's will. The first hurdle we face in discovering what God wants us to do is making room in our lives—our hearts—our homes—for God!*

> And this is my prayer: that your love may abound more and more in knowledge and in depth of insight, so that you may be able to discern what is best.[4]

## Waiting

*By Jane Kise*

The cheerless, gloomy isolation room at Children's Hospital where my 16-month-old daughter, Mari, and I had spent the night would be, it seemed, my home for at least 48 hours more. I stood by her crib, exhausted. She was safe now from the flu virus that had made her so ill, but her little body needed sleep. The doctor had told me that her muscles ached so much that she wouldn't want to be held or even touched.

I brushed a strand of hair from her forehead, checked that the life-giving IV was still in place, and wondered what to do next. I had to stay; my husband would patch together day care for Dan, our other pre-schooler. But what would I do while I waited?

Even the corridors seemed silent, especially compared with all of the comings and goings in the early-morning hours that had kept me from sleeping—although I hadn't expected to get much sleep in the vinyl-covered fold-out chair that doubled as a cot for parents.

I slumped back into the chair, the past 36 hours replaying in my mind. Actually, I hadn't been tired at all until now, despite a couple of sleepless nights. How had I managed to calmly remain with my daughter through the spinal tap, the X rays, and the long wait for results? *It was you, God, wasn't it? Thank you for your care, but what do I do now?*

With two children under the age of four, I never had enough time. While Mari slept, I could return all of those business phone calls, go over financial projections, or even work through some training materials without being interrupted. Better yet, I deserved a rest. What about reading a few of the novels on my nightstand?

In the chapel-like stillness of the room, I seemed to hear God say, *"This is your chance for a whole day with me. When was the last time you had more than fifteen minutes for prayer?"*

*Time for prayer . . . time to be still?* Why *not* take this unexpected day of inactivity and spend it with God?

A bit later at the nurse's insistence, I dashed home for my toothbrush and apples and clean clothes. I didn't let myself touch anything connected with work, or those novels. Instead, I tucked Andrew Murray's *The Believer's School of Prayer* into my overnight bag. I'd purchased it months before but hadn't had time to look past the table of contents.

Later that day, and all through the next, I settled into that vinyl chair, feet up, notebook by my side, and slowly underlined, looked up Scripture passages, and prayed. Instead of trying to finish the book, I let each thought it contained capture my attention until I felt moved to go on.

It wasn't until that evening that Mari sat up and called, "Mom? Mom!" Ever so gently, I picked her up, thankful that she again wanted to be hugged. As she laid her head on my shoulder and snuggled her nose into my neck, I whispered, "I know just how you feel." And I did, for during the past 24 hours, I'd felt that close to God.

As my prayers resonated with adoration and thankfulness for the Spirit's presence, I rejoiced in my God who could provide healing, peace, and renewal, even in a lumpy chair in a cheerless hospital room.

———————

*That day at the hospital changed permanently how close I felt to God. Shortly afterwards, I faced an incredibly difficult confrontation with a co-worker. God seemed to be right in the room with me, on my shoulder, when I asked for guidance.*

*While I don't always remember to pray as soon as I should, the hospital room, followed by the confrontation, taught me a key principle. If you want to find and follow God's will, you need to take time to get to know your Creator.*

## Cowboy Preacher Up
*Dave Kes*
*As told to Barbara Marshak*

I'm a businessman, a systems support technician, Monday through Friday. I'm a product of the suburbs; I grew up in a ranch home, not on a ranch. I'm as citified as a Midwesterner can be.

When Lindy and I married in 1994, we brought five kids to live together in our home in the suburbs. Both of us believed we'd been given a second chance to create a close family, with God at the center. As their stepfather, I vowed to show Josh and Isaac that I was interested in who they were and what they liked to do.

But bull riding? The idea certainly didn't come from Lindy or me!

When Josh, the oldest, first said, "I want to try bull riding," we were both firm in our answer: "No."

Or maybe it was a bit stronger, like, "Absolutely not." Was he insane?

Just like a stubborn cowboy, Josh dug in his heels and wouldn't let it go. He was 21; we shared our concerns but knew we couldn't really stop him. Eventually he started riding with his buddies at some of the smaller rodeos around rural Minnesota and developed a zeal for the dangerous sport. Despite our apprehension, Lindy felt compelled to watch Josh ride and I knew I needed to join her.

The atmosphere is dusty, dirty, and loud, with the announcer's microphone echoing and buzzers blaring across the grounds. But the anticipation of every rodeo builds toward the crowd favorite: bull riding!

Who'd have guessed that on the rodeo circuit there were specific names for bulls of different shapes, sizes, and moods:

Chute Fighter—*tries to fight the cowboy before he leaves the chute;*

Slinger—*tries to hit the cowboy with his head or horns while he's still on his back;*

Trash—*a bull with no set pattern;*

Head Hunter—*constantly looking for a two-legged target;*

Jump & Kicker—*jumps and kicks its hind feet in a straightaway action.*

To me, all those different names just spelled trouble. Talk about a mother's worst nightmare (or a stepfather's), to watch her young son voluntarily swing his body onto the back of 1,800 pounds of fightin' fury. When the chute opens and the angry animal lunges into the arena, kicking, twisting, and bucking, it hardly seems fair that the contestant has to hang on with only one hand. Watching Josh in the chute, his hand shaking as he worked it under the rope, I saw the fear and adrenaline etched on his face. Instantly I started praying for him. Eight seconds never seemed so long!

Our hearts in our mouths, we continued attending Josh's rodeos. By the next year his younger brother, Isaac, 18, was joining him.

When Lindy couldn't go because of the other children's activities, I went without her. Instead of heading to the spectator bleachers, I was drawn to the back of the arena where the bull riders prepared for their event. I waited along the corral, watching the line of lanky young men in Wrangler blue jeans, crisply ironed shirts, and wide-brimmed cowboy hats going through their rituals. Rosining up the ropes, getting them good and sticky—right on down the row, each one took care of his own equipment.

That's the physical part.

Then there's the psychological aspect: gathering the courage to climb on and give it your all. There was a name for that, too: *Cowboy Up.*

*But they need more than that,* I realized one afternoon as I listened to the bulls snort and stamp a few feet away. *They need more than my silent prayers as the chute opens; they need to* hear *me pray.* I called Josh and Isaac aside and told them I wanted to pray with them before they rode. They shrugged and said, "Sure."

As I bowed my head, I heard God's voice say, *"You've got two boys here, but I've got a whole lot more."*

*Are you kidding? The other riders? They'll brush me off as fast as I'd be bucked off one of those bulls!* But God's voice was distinct and clear. *"Do it."*

*I'm not a cowboy, God,* I argued in all honesty. *I can't connect with these boys.* I glanced at the young faces, bright with excitement, skittish of the unknown, and my urge to resist God drained away. *You're serious about this, aren't you, Lord. . . . If they have the courage to ride these big bulls, I can do this much. I'll obey.*

Nervously I wiped my hands on my jeans and took a step toward the first young man, a blond kid about 20 years old with a crooked grin and a bold plaid shirt.

"Say," I started, clearing my throat. "Well, we're gonna pray down there in a minute if you want to join us," I said, avoiding any eye contact. I hurried down the line, repeating myself as I walked, still averting my eyes.

There, I'd met the minimum requirements of obedience. I walked back to Josh and Isaac and bent down on one knee. As I worked my way into that first prayer, suddenly the words just came, as if God had taken over. When I glanced up, fifteen guys were crowded around us. My eyes filled with tears of thankfulness that I'd listened to God's command.

That's how it started. I said, "Okay, God," and before I knew it I had a ministry. From that day on I invited all the bull riders to join us in prayer before they rode.

Then . . . I prayed about how to make this ministry better. One weekend it was 95 degrees out and humid, so I filled a cooler with water bottles and ice and brought it along. It was a magnet, a perfect opportunity to pull the men together, share a couple verses, and offer a bit of insight.

Another time a cowboy had a *bad wreck* (seriously painful buck off, followed by getting horned or stomped). This young kid's family lived a couple hundred miles away, so I went to the hospital to wait it out with him. When he came to, his eyes showed how thankful he was to see a familiar face.

The next season I took it one step further, following one particular circuit, even though Josh and Isaac were riding elsewhere. Lindy and I worked it out ahead of time, deciding which weekends she needed me at home.

When a cowboy comes up to me and says, "Dave, your prayers make me feel like there's a reassuring hand on my shoulder," I'm sure that God is drawing him a bit closer. I don't always know where some of these young men are spiritually, but my ministry isn't a sprint where everything has to be done in a month.

That was six years ago. Now I routinely go wherever the National Federation of Professional Bullriders takes me. No one knows my last name; they just call me Preacher Dave. The cowboys joke that I travel more than they do, but I take that as a sign of trust. I'll be there when a young man lands in a hospital or invites me to his baptism. I'll come when I'm invited to give a cowboy church service. While I'm not an ordained pastor, whenever I doubt my calling, God reminds me that it's about backing up my words with actions. The bull riders know I'm not going to fade away. For now, I'm hanging around behind the chutes, waiting to see what God is going to do next.

---

*Both Dave and his wife, Lindy, have accepted this rodeo ministry as a true calling from God. Dave's new position at work has given him more flexibility in his schedule, allowing him to travel the long distances necessary on weekends. He knows it is another confirmation of God's leading. Today, Dave is much more comfortable in his role as God continues to provide more opportunities for his ministry each year.*

## When God Opened Our Doors
### By Gregg and Janet Anderson [5]

**Janet:** On an ordinary afternoon drive, I spotted a billboard that said, "Wanted: Loving Homes." Beneath a collage of children of all ages and backgrounds was the name and number of a foster-care agency. Since my teen years, I'd hoped to work with children in need.

"Foster care," I said, pointing out the sign to Gregg. "We've got room for—"

"No, no way. Raising three children is enough," was his instant reply. We'd been married over twenty years; I didn't try to argue. Instead, I prayed, *God, if foster care is your idea, let Gregg know.*

**Gregg:** And . . . two years later, we were driving home from a prayer service when I turned to Janet—I know exactly which intersection we were at—and said, "Let's check out foster care." Even as I spoke, I wondered, *Where did that come from?* The prayer service was about missions, not children.

I had to believe that God put those words in my mouth—*my* future plans included more fishing, more time for the two of us. Once I'd said it, though, I figured it'd let us use all we'd learned from parenting mistakes with our own children.

**Janet:** A child-protection worker who attended our church offered to explain what foster care *really* entailed, as he put it.

**Gregg:** That was an interesting conversation—stories about foster kids beating up foster parents, destroying personal property, starting fires, injuring neighbors, or breaking into their homes.

He told us, "Too many potential foster parents think that love will conquer all. Then they wake up to urine in their ductwork or their own children using drugs."

We were *sure* it'd be different at our house. God *told* us to do this!

**Janet:** I thought, *The children still need a place to grow or this world will never get better.*

**Gregg:** Our caseworker insisted that we start small. For a few months, two little girls joined our family every weekend. Suddenly, they stopped coming. We never learned why. That's the reality of foster care: You have little control over the children's future.

**Janet:** Not even for small things. Right now we're caring for two little boys. The one-year-old has gorgeous curly hair that's a magnet for his older brother to yank. I want to trim that baby's hair, but it's not my call.

From the start, we *thought* we'd turned over control, praying, "God, we will take any child you send here." I think God chose the next two boys to test us—they awoke at five each morning and never stopped running.

**Gregg:** Up one flight of stairs and down the other. Their feet didn't even touch the carpet—maybe they ran on the ceiling! "Three months we can handle," we told each other, "and then they'll be gone." But—they lived with us until they finished school! You never know.

**Janet:** We almost gave up with one boy, Robert. We couldn't seem to get through his anger. His first morning at church, Robert threw a huge tantrum in the parking lot. So I sat on the lawn, holding him tightly, as his case file recommended, while he shrieked and cursed at me, the church, and our friends who walked by. They all smiled, saying, "Good morning." They understood.

After weeks of this, Gregg and I prayed, "God, Robert doesn't respond to us." Our own words came back, *"We'll take any child that you send us."* So we kept trying, reminding each other of that promise multiple times each day. And slowly things changed. . . . Robert was the first child we adopted!

**Gregg:** We adopted two. Five more stayed with us until they turned 18. We've never asked to have a child removed, but our caseworker decided to place a few elsewhere. One boy punched through walls, ran away—I've never seen such hatred or lack of conscience.

One night we'd headed out for a motorcycle ride—two dear friends baby-sit for us every Monday—when our cell phone rang. This boy had climbed onto the roof of our two-story home, in the rain. Before they could "capture" him, he bolted down the street.

We told our friends to call the police. When they caught him, his screams brought half the neighborhood outside, even in the rain.

Our friends said they didn't think they could baby-sit again until he was gone.

**Janet:** But we keep praying for those children after they've left. We pray every night while they're here, too, whether they join in or not.

One night I stood at the doorway of the girls' room, saying bedtime prayers. The newest arrival kept singing and talking as I prayed. Finally the girl next to her, who hadn't really shown interest in prayers before, said, "Get some respect! Can't you hear what she's doing?"

So you never know what seeds you're planting.

**Gregg:** We've been spared from the worst kinds of problems. I like to tell people we have a couple of very large angels with swords sitting up on top of the roof. And they just . . . nobody messes around here.

**Janet:** For several years we only took children with "high difficulty-of-care assessments:" ADHD, EBD, PTSD, autism, or a life-threatening eating disorder. With those children, numbers didn't matter—sometimes three were more work than ten.

When high-needs children became our focus, I remember thinking that they'd need more structure and routine. I'm an in-the-moment person—disorganized would describe it better. I can't plan my way out of a paper bag! Who was I to think I could give these kids what they needed to feel safe?

Then one day I mentioned our newest arrival to a friend. She said, "How can you stand sudden arrivals—didn't your plans for the weekend get thrown off?"

"I hadn't made any yet," I replied. Then it struck me—as a foster parent, you *have* to go with the flow. My biggest strength in this work comes from my biggest weakness. Planning meals for a week is futile if you don't know how many mouths you'll have to feed. Instead, we have three freezers filled for whoever is here!

**Gregg:** You never think of chaos as a strength, but it's perfect for running a shelter.

For me . . . as a kid, I was a master manipulator. I was *horrible*, daring my brothers to do all kinds of things and watching them get into trouble. My devious past helps me anticipate what our foster kids might do. One night I had a hunch about a couple of the boys, so I took my post outside the girls' room. Sure enough, they came sneaking up—one had dared the other to pull a prank. "How did you know what we were doing?" the instigator said.

"Because I tried that, too, when I was your age!"

The fact that God uses our weaknesses tells you how much we do *not* deserve credit for what happens in our home. We would have quit long ago if we'd been relying on ourselves.

**Janet:** Although last year we had new troubles. Gregg's parents came to live with us. They had their own apartment, but they had needs as well. Our adopted daughter, Kelly, began grieving intensely when kids who'd been here for months suddenly moved on. She insisted we adopt them all.

**Gregg:** It's not that we didn't realize Kelly's or my parents' needs. Instead . . . I can't put my finger on when—at first we *were* planning how many children to take, and how to be licensed—but somewhere in our twelve years of foster care we stopped planning and said, "God, just let us know what you want us to do next. Your plans are better than ours."

**Janet:** And God's plan was for us to switch to shelter care. Children arrive on a moment's notice, but they only stay a few weeks at most. And you're required to close down for four weeks of the year—a real vacation! It's perfect for Kelly and Gregg's parents.

**Gregg:** But with shelter—we had 54 different children in the first three months of the year—I questioned God about what we were really accomplishing. And it kept coming back, *Some people plant seeds . . . some cultivate. You're planting seeds right now.* And hopefully something will sink in, they'll see that they can make better choices for their own children.

As for what's next? We're well past our fiftieth birthdays. Eventually we'll be too old to do shelter care.

**Janet:** You never know. We might change the age group we work with. Or we could go back to longer-term care with fewer children.

**Gregg:** There *are* adult programs, too. There's a couple in their 90s who are taking care of 70-year-old adults with disabilities! We're not worried—God keeps showing us what to do next!

———

*Gregg and Janet say they could not run their shelter without the help of their friends who baby-sit every Monday, their daughter who backs them up at a moment's notice, and their church family who accepts the unique needs and quirks of all of the children they care for. They also know that many people—family, church friends, and friends of friends—pray for their work. While foster care isn't for everyone, they hope their story might encourage more people to reach out and support foster families.*

## KEY: The first step in finding God's will is giving our lives to God.

"I wish God would just tell me what to do."

When I find myself asking that question I stop and take inventory, "Would I recognize God's voice if I heard it? Have I listened for it lately?"

My prayer life is far from perfect, but I keep my journal and devotional book in my window-seat prayer spot, along with a coaster for my coffee mug. The spot calls, *Listen to God, make that your top priority,* no matter how many deadlines I'm facing or how many events crowd our family calendar. If I don't take the time, eventually I make a mistake, a slap-in-the-face reminder that I haven't been looking for direction.

Preacher Dave, the foster-care family—they were listening for God's voice. They might not have been asking, "Should I pray with the rodeo riders?" but they were in conversation. Finding God's will isn't like hide-and-seek or cat and mouse—it isn't a secret, but something that God reveals to us if we're prepared to understand it.

Think of it this way: Why would anyone follow someone they don't know? If they've only seen the person from a distance, or heard stories from someone else, can they even be positive they're tagging the right individual?

The same is true of following God. While our Creator does speak to people who aren't looking for direction (remember Samuel, as a young boy, being awakened by God's voice in 1 Samuel 3?), discovering what God wants you to do is definitely easier if you take the time to recognize the voice of the One you would follow.

*Lord, if I knew you better, would I*
*trust your guiding hand?*
    *hear your call?*
        *obey your voice?*
*Help me draw closer,*
    *Until I grasp*
        *that the safest way to go*
*is down the path you want me to follow. Amen.*

---

[1]Psalm 137:1
[2]Isaiah 53:5
[3]Philippians 2:7, 10–11
[4]Philippians 1:9
[5]All names in this story have been changed to protect the anonymity of Janet and Gregg's shelter and the children they serve.

# 2

# What If I'm Just Not Sure What to Do?

Key: God's will is about faith, not certainty.

*Even if you've never farmed, you've seen pictures. Weeks of heavy labor. Constant anxiety about the weather. Relief when the crops are safely to market or stored away. A successful harvest is reason for celebration in agricultural societies worldwide.*

*But what if someone stole that entire harvest? Let you do all that work and then robbed you of the fruit of your labor?*

*That's what the people of Midian did to the Israelites for seven years in a row, taking not just their food supply but seeds for the next planting. Most Israelites had given up; they simply hid in caves rather than face the Midianites.*

*But not everyone. Let's meet Gideon. . . .*

---

*Crack. Thump. Rustle.* Gideon raised the flail over his head and brought it down again on the bundle of sheaves he'd managed to carry home from the fields. He paused for a moment, wiping the sweat from his forehead before pulling more grass from the pile. He couldn't help but think of past harvests, walking behind the oxen on their hilltop threshing floor while the breeze swept away the dust and chaff. Now here he was, down in a stone pit, like a rabbit avoiding the fox. *Whoops, don't swing so high or someone might spot you,* he reminded himself. He felt like a coward, but at least he hadn't left his crops for the taking, hiding in the hills like so many of his neighbors.

Choking on dust at the bottom of a pit was the only strategy he'd come up with to protect his family's meager harvest. The raiders would never look for him here; the grape season was months away. As the debris swirled off the stone walls and into Gideon's eyes, he kicked at the grain, then swung the flail again.

The raids had started a few years before. They rode in on camels, like clouds of locusts, similarly stripping the land and taking away Israel's hope as well as their grain. Some of the men in town swore that the Midianites were more than a hundred thousand strong—how could Israel be safe again? *Don't think . . . just thresh the wheat.*

So intent was he on his task that he didn't notice a figure appear under a nearby oak tree. A voice startled him, "The Lord is with you, mighty warrior."

Gideon whirled around, expecting raiders. Instead, seated there was a solitary stranger, calm and smiling, with unsoiled robes. Obviously this person hadn't been harvesting or hiding in the hills. Gideon wondered, *Is he mocking me? I'm hardly warrior material, cowering in the bottom of a pit.*

"The Lord is with us?" spilled out of Gideon's mouth. "As we live in terror of the Midianites? If this is how we fare under the God who rescued Moses, it seems more like God abandoned us."

The man stood up, suddenly taller, his robes whiter. Gideon took a step back, his heart thudding in his chest. The blood drained from his hot, dusty face. Who was this man?

As the man leaned toward Gideon, he said, "You have the strength to save Israel. I'm sending you."

"M-me?" Gideon sputtered. "But my clan is the weakest in all of Israel—and I'm the youngest in the whole family!"

The man ignored Gideon's words and went on. "I am with you. You will strike down the Midianites one and all."

Images of hordes of camels and swords crowded Gideon's mind. The walls of the winepress seemed to reel as he struggled to make sense of the man's words. The wisest, most experienced soldiers in the village had failed to defend their fields, let alone conquer the enemy or even deter the raids. The man talked nonsense.

But who was he? No one from here. The spotless robes, the peaceful gaze of his eyes . . . Was this truly a messenger from God? How could he be sure? Gideon knelt down. "If somehow the Lord has truly found me worthy of such a task, please give me a sign. Stay, please, while I prepare an offering to you."

"I will wait for your return."

Heart pounding, hands shaking, mind pulsing with questions, Gideon stumbled up the path to his father's house. What was happening? Why would God stop by a winepress? *Think, Gideon, slow down. This offering must be perfect.*

He worked quickly, but hours passed before he could properly prepare meat and broth from a young goat, fashion unleavened loaves of bread, and carry everything back to where the man waited under the oak.

When Gideon approached, the angel said, "Place the meat and bread here, on this rock, and pour out the broth."

Gideon followed the instructions, then watched in awe as fire flared from the rock, consuming the meat and bread. He exclaimed, "I have seen an angel of the Lord face-to-face!"

———

*Gideon's story is all too often used as a model for how to seek God's guidance, rather than as an example of how God guides those who are called to monumental tasks. God was asking Gideon to risk not just his own life but the lives of all who followed him into battle.*

*That fire from the rock gave Gideon the courage he needed to tear down the altars to other gods that the townspeople had built. Later, when God asked him to lead an actual attack on the Midianites, Gideon asked for two more signs: that when he spread a fleece out on the ground, God would dampen the fleece while the ground remained dry one night, then keep the fleece dry while the surrounding ground became covered in dew the next.*

*While the Bible is filled with examples of this kind of clear-cut guidance, before you test God by "putting out a fleece" consider whether you really want to undertake the kinds of actions the Bible heroes so guided were asked to perform. Leading an army, like Gideon? Being summoned by a burning bush, like Moses, so you can take God's truth before the leader of a huge nation? If not, what kind of guidance can you expect?*

*In each of the following stories, you'll read of people who faced very, very difficult situations. God seemed to give them just enough assurance to keep moving—which, given the dangers involved, is probably all Gideon got in the way of assurance as well. They still had to walk forward in faith, not certainty.*

Now faith is being sure of what we hope for and certain of what we do not see.[1]

## A Sister's Promise

*Harriette Peterson Koopman*
*As told by daughter, Connie Pettersen*

December 7, 1941. I was almost 18 when bombs fell on Pearl Harbor. My older brothers, Orv and Bob, enlisted in the army during the heartfelt wave of patriotism that swept across America, making me the eldest of seven kids at home.

My closest sibling and best friend was Don, two years younger. Linked by common interests—singing, laughing, and playing jokes on each other—we were close confidantes, keeping secrets safe no matter what.

Just like homemade cider and fudge stirred up together, Don's and my relationship was warm, sweet, comforting. He and I jitterbugged around the kitchen during dishes, drumming wooden spoons against a kettle and snapping each other with wet dish towels. Our teenage voices echoed through the house as we harmonized with the radio's popular war songs like, "Don't Sit Under the Apple Tree With Anyone Else but Me" and "I'll Be Seeing You." Don's favorite was "Put My Little Shoes Away," an old folk song about heaven.

After every letter from Orv or Bob, Don wanted to enlist. One night in the kitchen, he begged Pa to let him join the navy.

"I wanna go, Pa . . . my country needs me."

Pa's face turned ashen. "You're not old enough!"

"When I'm seventeen, you could sign—"

"No! This war has *two* of my boys." Pa left the room. *Thank you, God,* I thought. How could I stand having another brother so far away and in such danger?

Don persisted for months, though, wearing at my parents' patience. He reminded Ma that they needed the money he'd send home. Eventually she supported Don's enlistment. Still, Pa refused. Finally, after Don threatened to lie about his age, Pa agreed. Don joined the navy on his seventeenth birthday, November 3, 1942.

That night he and I sat by the fire. I could scarcely breathe; the lump in my throat swelled so much. "Don, *please*. Don't go," I said.

"I have to, Sis. If our guys don't enlist, we'll never win. God's hand is in this war. It'll all work out."

He seemed so sure. So grown up. *He's trusting in God, why can't you?* I asked myself. Finally I reached for his hand. "Then I'll send you 'On a Wing and a Prayer,'" I said, referring to the popular song.

Don became an aerial gunner with VB 112, a navy squadron flying PB4Ys. Without his laugh and gentle spirit the kitchen seemed too quiet, even when younger siblings helped. Every night I'd ask God to send an angel to watch over him. Don's letters home asked about family, friends, my new defense job, always closing with, "Sis . . . I'm in God's hands."

Don had one last leave with us before being deployed overseas. One night, our folks went dancing while Don and I baby-sat. As I frolicked with the kids on the braided living-room rug, Don sang and played "Put My Little Shoes Away" on the record player he'd sent home as a gift to the family.

Mother, I will be an angel
Perhaps before another day
So, you will then, dearest Mother
Put my little shoes away?

As Don played the record repeatedly, his thoughts were far away. "Don . . . are you okay?" I asked. "Don't you like the navy?"

"I like the navy. It's not that . . ."

After the kids were asleep we sat on the couch. "All right, if it's not the navy, what's wrong? Why aren't you with friends?"

Don hesitated. "Sis, you gotta promise . . . you can't tell Ma and Pa, it has to be a secret."

*A secret. Just like old times.* I nodded, wide-eyed, not knowing what to expect.

"Sis, I won't be coming home again. I'll be—I'll be giving my life for my country."

My face grew hot even as a chill coursed through my spine. "But how can you *know* that?"

"It's a feeling, a premonition. The Lord's given me peace about it."

*A peace? About dying at seventeen?* I didn't understand. Waiting for Don to continue, I searched his eyes for clues of his thoughts. Although they glistened with unshed tears, he sat with shoulders squared in military determination. His face showed pride and fierce loyalty to our country. He looked at me with calm acceptance etched into his face.

"Sis, we are at war with a grave enemy. We . . . don't know the outcome, we can only trust and put ourselves into God's hands."

Then I understood. Don would do his duty no matter what the personal cost. I bit my lip to stop its trembling. "If that's what you believe . . . stay close to the Lord. Don't let go!"

"I will," he promised. "That's why I want to take in as much of home as I can. Don't tell the folks, Sis. It'd kill Pa that he signed me in early."

I gave my word. We closed our eyes and prayed. My throat swelled. I couldn't speak, nor could Don. Instead, we rested our foreheads together, embracing, tears mingling as we sought God's comfort.

Days later, we gathered around Don at the train station, one by one tearfully hugging him good-bye. When my turn came, a favorite hymn we'd sung together filled my thoughts. With a quivering voice, I began:

*God be with you till we meet again.*
*When life's perils thick confound you . . .*

Don grabbed my hand, squeezed it tight, and joined me on the chorus.

The conductor yelled the last call. "Booooo-rd. All A-booooord."

Don took a deep breath. With tears streaming down his face, he turned and ran for the train. He didn't look back.

A few weeks later my father moved the family to Oregon to begin his defense industry job welding battleships. I wasn't allowed to leave my defense job at International Harvester in St. Paul. *If Don can do his job, knowing God is with him, so can I,* I told myself as I faced life without the family that had always surrounded me.

On his eighteenth birthday, November 3, 1943, Don shipped overseas to French Morocco. He took his post as an ordnance man and gunner on a B–24 Liberator. On Don's first combat mission, November 30, 1943, Don's plane crashed into the Mediterranean Sea. As I'd promised, I kept our secret rather than add to our folks' guilt for allowing him to enlist at seventeen.

I don't know why God let Don know he would die—many people wouldn't want to know—but I'm sure of two things. First, Don held on to that peace I'd seen in his face, knowing heaven was his real home, even as his plane went down. Second, throughout my life I've held on to the lesson Don's faith taught me: If I think I'm following God's lead, I don't need all the answers even if the path seems headed for the darkest of dark places. God will be with me.

Sixty years later, I know Don won't mind if I share his secret. He was a brave American, a wonderful brother, and faithful Christian. He taught me to trust the Lord in everything, no matter what. I look forward to heaven with the same assurance I saw in my brother's face on his last leave home. I picture the day Don and I will once again sing together:

Till we meet . . . at Jesus' feet . . .
God be with you . . . till we meet again.

---

*Connie's note:*

After Don's death, a family-hardship release allowed Mom to leave her defense job and move to Portland where she became active in church work with a deaconess, Helen Michelke.

In August 1945, Mom accepted an invitation to accompany Helen on a visit to their family farm in South Dakota where my parents met. Their marriage lasted 48 years. Mom told me Don's confidence in trusting God in all things gave her courage to leave St. Paul, throw herself into church work, and take the path that led to Dad and their life together.

The official military letters sent to my grandparents after Don's death gave little information; one stated Don was "radio operator," another said "weapons specialist."

I felt led to research this family mystery 59 years later. A navy Web site provided details of the crash, listing names of deceased crew and survivors. I contacted a survivor, Mr. Lyle Van Hook, Don's flight officer, who e-mailed his account of the crash:

"Don had been weapons ordinance specialist and tail gunner. Their radio operator (also killed in the crash) had repeatedly—unsuccessfully—

tried to radio their base. In dense night fog, their squadron was returning from a successful Atlantic patrol mission guarding U.S. convoys to Italy. Critically low on fuel, their plane crashed within sight of the southern coast of Faro, Portugal. The impact broke the plane apart, killing five crew members. Six survivors were pulled from the sea and into a small boat guided by two Portuguese fishermen."

Mr. Van Hook remembered Don well and appreciated learning that Don's faith had been strong, although he wasn't surprised. Don's face reflected a determined calmness that night. Van Hook also said the plane's wreckage had been found by divers.

Learning the details after so many years gave my mom a renewed connection with her closest brother, and Mr. Van Hook has become a family friend.

Somehow, I think Uncle Don approves.

## How Can I Ask?
*By Rhonda Jensen*

Lilacs for a June wedding, just as I'd always wanted. Their delicate aroma filled the church, radiating from my bouquet and the sprays adorning each pew. *This isn't a dream,* their fragrance sang to me. *You made it!*

I smiled at Kevin, so handsome in his tux. He'd stayed by my side during my long battle with leukemia. A month before my bone marrow transplant, he'd knelt beside my hospital bed and slipped an engagement ring on my finger. Even the transplant only gave me a 20 percent chance of making it. But I had. And here we were, thanks to Elly, the woman who'd donated her bone marrow to a total stranger—me.

I prayed, *God, thank you for touching Elly's heart.* I'd tucked tissues into Bailey's flower-girl basket, and I needed them. At the altar Kevin squeezed my hand tightly, yet the tears came. No sign of leukemia in over three years. I'd had a hip replaced several months before, made necessary by my body's reaction to anti-rejection drugs. But that surgery gave relief from constant pain. I couldn't wait to have the other hip done.

I'd only been off of crutches for a few weeks; my sister had to rub ointment on my sore muscles partway through the reception. But I didn't want to stop celebrating. Of all brides, I felt most truly blessed.

Radiant as I was that day, my health wasn't perfect. My kidneys, damaged by radiation treatments and anti-rejection drugs, only worked at about 30 percent capacity. For years, I'd restricted my intake of milk, orange juice, bananas, cheese, and tomatoes. Kevin joked about the scarcity of pasta toppings.

Later that summer, a routine exam showed that my kidneys were down to around 10 percent. "It isn't an emergency," the specialist said, "but it's time you knew your options."

I could make the hour-long trek to Wausau three times a week for dialysis for the next twenty years or so. I could have an abdominal implant for home dialysis, but it would need to be changed frequently.

Or I could have a kidney transplant. My sister Brenda was the closest match. Together we met with the transplant doctor. "The surgery is usually harder on the donor than the recipient," he explained to Brenda. "You may lose a rib, the scar can be nearly a foot long, and there's danger if your remaining kidney is ever damaged."

"It'd be worth it," Brenda said firmly.

"But remember, you're not a perfect match." He turned to me. "Because the two of you only match on three of the six HLA sites, you'd need to take at least three medications for the rest of your life. Prednisone, the drug that damaged your hips, is one of them."

"So . . . I might need elbow transplants next?" I said, trying to smile.

"It's hard to tell. Too bad you don't know your bone marrow donor. That would be the ultimate kidney match."

My stomach flip-flopped. "She lives near Brenda!"

The doctor stared at me. "You have virtually the same immune systems. You wouldn't need anti-rejection drugs."

My mouth felt too dry to speak. "There is no way I could ask Elly for a kidney. She's already saved my life."

Brenda and I were both pretty quiet on the drive home. How could I ask any more of Elly, especially given the risks this time around? She worked on a farm; a bad fall could easily damage her remaining kidney.

Besides, Elly was a giver, quiet and humble. I'd first met her at the bridal shower my sisters had held for me. How Elly had blushed when she appeared from the spare bedroom and Brenda announced, "Here's the other guest of honor today."

Elly'd had struggles of her own. She'd been a single mother to three boys before marrying Randy, her second husband. She'd worked two, even three jobs to make ends meet. The four of us went out to dinner on each anniversary of the bone marrow transplant. Elly insisted, "Helping you helped me, too. It happened just when I was feeling like a failure at everything."

Brenda seemed to sense my thoughts. "I'd give you a kidney in an instant, but the drug issues . . . Elly won't say yes without researching and praying about it. She isn't the sort to be pressured into doing anything."

I shook my head.

"Think of it this way," she added slowly. "What if you *don't* ask and ten years from now those elbow replacements you joked about become a reality, or the dialysis grows less effective? It's your *life* we're talking about."

"It's Elly's life, too . . . and the doctor said I have months to decide, a few months, at any rate."

Over the next month I prayed and prayed. I'd start with, "God, these aren't fair choices." Then my thoughts whirled among the alternatives. Most days I finished with, "I guess you know what I mean . . . please help me know what to do."

When Brenda called again, insisting that I'd second-guess myself forever, I knew she was right. But how to ask? *God, I want Elly to be able to say no.* A letter seemed too impersonal, yet calling or meeting with Elly would put her on the spot. I asked Helen, the transplant coordinator, who suggested writing a letter. "Put my name and number in it. I'll make sure she can say no."

Countless times over the next few months, I stared at sheets of paper, not knowing what to say. Finally in January, I wrapped up in my favorite comforter and sat down on the couch with a blank tablet. I began with some general news to fill the gap since we'd last talked. *Kevin bought another dump truck, so now we have an employee and I am being kept busy with bookwork . . . I'm substitute teaching . . . in one month it will have been five years since the bone marrow transplant!*

Then I just laid out the facts. I gave Helen's number and concluded, *I feel bad presenting you with my situation when you have already done so much for me. But I felt that for my own peace of mind, I had to at least inform you of it and give you the option to decide if this would be something you would be willing to do . . . I am just considering all my options that the doctors presented me and praying that God keeps taking care of me.*

I read the letter out loud to Brenda, reread it ten thousand times, and dropped it in the mail. That was that. The outcome was up to Elly and God. Elly already had given me an extra twenty years of life, even if I would spend most of it on dialysis.

Brenda asked me within the week, "Did she call? Have you heard anything?"

"She can have as much time as she wants," I replied firmly. Meanwhile, I kept myself busy with work. I didn't need dialysis as long as I felt fine.

Late one morning, just a few minutes before I was leaving to teach, the postman delivered a box from Elly. Carefully I opened the flaps and caught a glimpse of lavender. A delicate bouquet of silk lilacs. Elly's favorite flower, and mine. A note tucked inside contained just a few words. I took a deep breath, then read *I wanted you to know that I've made my decision, but I need to convince my family, so pray for me.*

I read it again, then again, then at least a dozen times more. I hadn't expected Elly to say yes, yet here it was. Tears rolled down my face. *Pull yourself together, you have to go teach! Oh, what if something goes wrong for her?* I had to call right away.

When Elly answered her phone, my voice choked with relief, with wonder, with gratitude.

I asked whether she was sure. Elly said firmly, "Rhonda, last time, when I saw the picture of the needle they use for bone marrow extraction, I nearly backed out—I didn't know they *made* needles that big. My stomach churned for weeks. I was shaking so badly in the operating room that they gave me a mild sedative!

"But this time? Nothing I learned bothered me. That's when I knew that God wanted me to do this. I *didn't* feel pressured. Helen told me she'd find a medical reason if I wanted to say no."

Elly scheduled the necessary physical and psychological tests. A couple of weeks later she called and asked, "Are you busy on May 5? I've got two rooms reserved for us."

On May 6, a little shaky from the surgery, Elly walked into my hospital room, her nurse right behind her.

"You look better already," she said, reaching for my hand.

"You look like an angel, even with that hospital gown covering your wings," I replied. "I'm so thankful God made someone like you, so giving."

That was in 1999. Each day I remind myself to do the best I can with the time I've been given, listening for God's direction, looking for God's guidance as I did in writing to Elly. The best thing about life is being alive, a precious gift from God. Thanks to Elly, I've received that gift two more times.

---

*Rhonda's good health continues and she's been busy doing long-term subbing for teachers on maternity leave. She and Elly see each other at Christmas, but their transplant anniversary dinners are harder to schedule because Rhonda's family and others want to join in the celebration now. Rhonda and Elly also keep in touch through e-mail as well as Brenda's occasional conversations with Elly at the Mondovi grocery store and other places in town. Rhonda says that her amazement and thankfulness is renewed each day, that God brought someone as giving as Elly into her life.*

## A Birthday Blessing
*By Sheila McKinley*

My hands trembled as I wrapped my son Matthew's presents. Today was his fourth birthday. Sadness overwhelmed me as I remembered his party the year before. Then, I'd prayed that he'd understand it was his special day, but it hadn't happened.

Matthew has fragile X syndrome, a genetic condition with no cure. Delayed speech, attention problems, hyperactivity, learning disabilities, and repetitive gestures such as hand flapping are just some of his symptoms.

Simplicity works best for my son. For his third birthday, I had only invited my closest family and friends, and just one of Matthew's playmates. Matthew showed little interest in his guests or his presents. My sister tried to help him unwrap his gifts, but his attention span was too short. He kept wandering off to other parts of the room, staring at balloons, or trailing his little friend. I'd carefully decorated his cake with sugary images of his favorite television characters and topped it with a big candle shaped like a three. With help from his guests, Matthew blew out the candle but didn't seem to understand that it was *his* cake, *his* party. That night I prayed even more fervently, "Lord, will he ever talk, ever call me Mom? I need your help, your strength, and wisdom to teach him about life."

Now, a year later, wrapping more presents, I wondered what this party would bring. The sweet Matthew I saw so often who loved to give hugs? Or the boy with fragile X who struggled with transitions and unstructured situations?

I shuddered as I remembered a trip to the grocery store shortly after he turned three. I hadn't been able to understand what he needed from his grunts and tugs on my shirtsleeve. Finally he began screaming in frustration. Everyone in the grocery store glared at me, their eyes shouting unspoken words. *For shame, such a big boy throwing a tantrum. Did she hurt him somehow, he's screaming so loudly? If she can't handle him, she should leave him at home!* I wanted to scream back, "He has fragile X syndrome and I'm a single mother. Why don't you help instead of gawking at us?"

Instead, I focused on Matthew, rubbing his back as I repeated with a calmness I didn't feel, "Honey, I'm so sorry. I don't understand what you want." His frantic screams continued as I pushed the cart, filled with the milk and bread we desperately needed, toward a cashier.

My hands shook as I wrote the check, keeping my head down to avoid the clerk's angry expression. *You don't want me out of here half as much as I wish I could disappear,* I thought. When I was finally back in the car, I crossed my arms over the steering wheel and cried, *God, you have to help me help Matthew.*

What a year it had been. A few days after the grocery-store incident, I hooked a little harness around my son and walked with him toward the school bus stop. He'd never gone anywhere without me before, but he was old enough now to get speech therapy as well as help with social and emotional development. And the harness? I couldn't let myself care what people thought. He'd tried to run from me too many times, and the upshot of most chases was another tantrum. The bus driver must have seen worried mothers before. "He'll have a good day, ma'am. Don't you fret."

I'd taken a slow, tear-filled walk back to our apartment. The driver was right. That's what I needed to do, stop worrying and trust God. *Lord, keep*

*Matthew safe and help him learn today. And help me learn to trust you more.*

The sound of the doorbell brought me back to the present, a year later and another party. I sighed, taping the last piece of wrapping paper into place. Good things *had* happened over the past twelve months. Matthew loved his school. They used pictures to help him communicate and he had learned several words. One evening as he snuggled with me in the rocking chair, our bedtime routine, he began to softly sing, "Jesus loves me, this I know . . ."

Just weeks ago, as I unsnapped his harness at the school bus, he looked up at me and said clearly, "Mommy, I love you." Words I never thought I'd hear. I cried on that day, too.

But last week had been one of the toughest of Matthew's little life. He'd awakened one morning with a high fever. It went down during the day, then spiked again. When he started vomiting the next afternoon, I headed for the emergency room. "He's severely dehydrated," they told me.

First a nurse, then a doctor tried to get the IV started, without success. With each new attempt, Matthew screamed louder. I prayed, I sang, "Jesus Loves Me" to soothe him, but he became more hysterical. Finally a nurse asked, "Could we get him something to drink?" A glass of soda calmed him down. When he slept, I'd made calls from the emergency room to friends and family to cancel his birthday party scheduled for the next day.

Now, a week later, I was trying again. The day was actually nicer than the original party date, not as cold. Still, with Matthew I didn't know what the afternoon would bring. He'd recently been to a classmate's party and tried to unwrap all of *her* presents.

As the guests arrived, the little pile of gifts on my living room desk grew until it looked like Christmas. Matthew, in constant motion, trotted between the presents and the table that held a chocolate cake with candles shaped like toy cars. When the last guest arrived, I lit the four candles on his cake and started in on "Happy Birthday," anxious to capture this part of the party on video while Matthew seemed happy.

He helped us sing, and I could hear the excitement in his voice. This time he blew out his own candles. A lump rose in my throat as he tore open the paper on his presents all by himself, whooping and clapping even before he knew what was in it. He never lost interest.

When the last guest left Matthew tugged on my sleeve. I looked down, praying I'd understand what he wanted to tell me. His eyes shining, he said, "Mommy, thank you for my party," as clearly as anything he'd ever said to me.

My prayers of the year before, that Matthew would understand that it was his special day, had been answered. But the day was even more special to me. Seeing his joy helped me appreciate how far he—and I—had come in a year. It was as if God put an extra dose of joy in my son for his fourth birthday to tell me, *I know you're doing the best that you can. I'm with you, even when you aren't sure what to do next.*

I've held to that message, trusting God even though I'm not sure what Matthew's future holds. Whenever I start worrying, I pull out the memory of Matthew ripping into his birthday presents, reliving the moment until I smile. *Sheila,* God seems to say, *trust me. I'm always here.*

———

*Sheila, a freelance writer and poet, reports that Matthew, now six, still loves school, although he does best with very structured activities. He can write his name and learns a new Bible verse each week through pictures. His first-grade teacher calls him her "shining star" and appreciates Matt's enthusiastic clapping for his classmates' accomplishments. He can now ask and answer some questions, but for Sheila, hearing the word Mom helps her remember the progress they've made. "Now he wants to open presents every day, but he's simply a great present to me," she says.*

## KEY: God's will is about faith, not certainty.

When the future seems fuzzy or overwhelming or forbidding, we may need to move ahead to discover what to do. Picture yourself in the driver's seat of a car. No matter how hard you crank the wheels, you can't change the direction it's pointed unless you first put it in gear. In gear, though, even if it's barely moving, even if the only propulsion comes from a few strong bodies pushing the vehicle from behind, turning the steering wheel will turn a moving car.

We can go slowly, as Rhonda did while pondering and worrying about whether she could possibly contact Elly. Sometimes like Don, we might rush ahead, knowing for certain that God is with us. And sometimes we're carried along by life, as was Sheila, her son's needs changing with each day. Fast or slow, moving ahead may be the only way to find the right path.

If you're afraid to take that first step, here are some thoughts to make it easier. Visualize that first step as a meandering rather than a commitment to one path. You might not get it quite right the first time, but you'll learn from each dead end. And at every moment along the way, you can ask God questions. Gideon did, as did each of our storytellers.

Still hesitant to try? Remember that the One you are following is a God of love, not of fear. Besides, the alternative is relying on your own sense of direction. God's plans are far safer than any scheme we could devise.

*Lord, sometimes every turn looks dangerous,*
*every alternative seems bleak.*
*Yet even as I hesitate*
*where I am seems to vanish.*
*I hear your plea, "Have faith in me."*
*Faith that you are with me . . .*
*I place my trust in you. Amen.*

---

[1]Hebrews 11:1

# 3

# What Can the Bible Tell Me Today?

Key: The Bible is still our sovereign source for discovering God's will.

*Are you comfortable with using the Bible, God's Word, to guide your life decisions? Some people refer to it as the instructions God gave us for living.*

*The Bible is full of God's wisdom, but as with anything, some people read instructions and some people don't. Further, the Bible was written long ago to people in very different circumstances. Open to certain passages and you might find justification for slavery, war, the oppression of women, or even that the heavens revolve around the earth—if you misuse God's Word.*

*The Bible itself, though, gives examples of how to use its pages wisely. In Acts 15, you can read about a dispute in the early church. Some leaders pointed to the laws of Moses and were sure that all new Christians needed to be circumcised. Scripture said so. Peter, Paul, and Barnabas disagreed. A council was called to decide the issue.*

---

James cast a quick look around the dimly lit room. The apostles and elders sat on stools, the floor, or simply leaned against the wall, their faces half hidden in the shadows cast by flickering oil lamps. The meeting was barely underway, yet already the small room grew warm. He shifted uneasily in his seat, still smarting from Paul's hot words of criticism the night before. *You've heard it from me, you heard it from Peter. God is working among the Gentiles. If they receive the Spirit, who are you, or anyone else to say they should have to follow each detail of the law? God has declared them clean. Can't you see that God is asking us to think differently?*

The anger directed at him from the elders on the other side of the issue was no less heated. Well, each side was now getting a chance to address the council.

His head ached. He'd been up half the night, praying, hoping God would speak to him, but instead his thoughts had twisted in knots. *Every male among you shall be circumcised . . .*[1] *Do not call anything impure that God has made clean . . .*[2] God seemed to be on both sides of the issue. The air in the crowded room grew more and more stale. He rubbed his forehead, trying to clear his mind. They needed to finish quickly or tempers would flare even more.

James had chosen a seat a bit off from the center so that he could watch everyone's faces. Those elders in favor of circumcision had spoken first. Now they sat across from him, tight-lipped, arms folded across their chests. Nothing anyone else said appeared to influence them, so sure were they that the law was on their side. "Remember how Moses' wife circumcised their son to avoid God's anger? The law applies to more than infants," they'd repeated.

Jesus' own words echoed in James's head, "Do not think that I have come to abolish the Law or the Prophets; I have not come to abolish them but to fulfill them. I tell you the truth, until heaven and earth disappear, not the smallest letter, not the least stroke of a pen, will by any means disappear from the Law until everything is accomplished."[3] How could he reconcile that with Paul's insistence that Gentiles need not be circumcised?

Peter spoke next. He cleared his throat, then waited patiently, smiling slightly, until the room grew still. "You've heard before how my ministry to the Gentiles began with Cornelius. Not once, but three times a cloth containing animals and reptiles and birds appeared to me. Three times a voice spoke and declared them all clean."

As Peter talked, he stared directly at the elders who insisted on circumcision. James watched their frowns deepen as Peter went on to describe the vision God had given him.

"That very day, God, who knows the heart, accepted the Gentiles by giving the Holy Spirit to them. Some of you were with me. You saw this." Murmurs of agreement wafted round the room. Peter nodded firmly. "If

God has already accepted them, who are we to insist on more?"

"We, too, have seen God working among the Gentiles," Barnabas added quietly, getting to his feet as Peter finished. The entire room grew still as first Barnabas, then Paul, shared stories of healing a lame man in Lystra, of new believers who had already stood up to persecution.

As the apostles finished and sat down, James caught snatches of conversations that broke out. "The Law is the *Law*." "Without being circumcised, could a Gentile be allowed to lead? Or even teach?"

*Gentiles . . .* another passage of Scripture flowed through James's thoughts. Suddenly James knew what to say. He stood and raised a hand. Quickly the crowd grew silent. James looked at the other leaders, then began, "Peter has shared how God first visited the Gentiles to select those who would bring honor to the name of our Lord. The prophet Amos foretold these events. Remember these words?

> After this I will return and rebuild David's fallen tent.
> Its ruins I will rebuild and I will restore it,
> that the remnant of men may seek the Lord,
> and all the Gentiles who bear my name."[4]

James looked around the room. Even the men who had insisted on circumcision looked thoughtful. He concluded slowly, "It is my judgment, then, that we shouldn't make it more difficult for Gentiles to turn to God."

---

*The fact that the church never debates the issue of circumcision tells how successfully the Council of Jerusalem settled this dispute. Note that both sides used Scripture, but the group that prevailed had a different view of God's Word.*

- *They searched the Scriptures from beginning to end. On some subjects—such as "thou shalt not kill"—the Bible is unchanging. On other subjects—circumcision, the day on which we worship, and others— the Bible changes between Genesis and Revelation. James looked to the books of the Prophets, not just the laws of Moses, and learned more about God's heart for the Gentiles.*
- *They considered other sources of wisdom. Peter had been led directly by God to go to the Gentiles (Acts 10). Barnabas and Paul had seen*

*results—Paul called their experiences an "open door" to bring the Gospel to the Gentiles.*

The Bible is a source of wisdom for today. The more you know about the Bible, the easier it is to understand how its wisdom applies to the dilemmas you face. In the next stories, see how God still speaks through the ancient pages of Scripture.

All Scripture is inspired by God and is useful for teaching, for reproof, for correction, and for training in righteousness, so that everyone who belongs to God may be proficient, equipped for every good work.[5]

## Fear Not
*By Brenda Henry*

My head rested on the back of the sofa as words from Isaiah meandered into my heart, plopped down, and made themselves comfortable. *This is what the Lord says . . . "Fear not, for I have redeemed you; I have summoned you by name; you are mine."* [6]

Hope sprung forth as their balmy presence encouraged the question: Could it be that a life completely free of fear is what God wants?

Every ounce of my being yelped the word "Yes!" as I imagined spending my days free from the paralyzing fear I'd experienced since girlhood. Prone to nightmares, I constantly feared the lurkers under my bed. Making sure my feet never came within three feet of its edge, I perfected a flying leap onto my soft mattress.

Night after night this same ritual brought assurance that nothing could grab my ankles and pull me into the black unknown that terrified me. Daylight brought relief from the shadowy spaces, but not from the unnerving sense that I was never safe. Even talking seemed risky sometimes. My words felt held back. Afraid to be the real me, I lived as a nervous person, void of my freedom of speech.

Years of living as a captive passed and there I sat, thirty-eight years old and paralyzed. Saddened by this false imprisonment and moved to break free, I began a voracious Scripture search of both the Old and New Testament. One morning my attention fell upon the fellow in John 5 who sat beside the pool of Bethesda for thirty-eight years, unable to get in. When Jesus healed him, this paralyzed man jumped off the thin, fragile pages of my Bible and a gentle whisper nudged, *That's you, child. That's you. Do you want to get up?* I did, but I wasn't sure how. I only knew I could no longer ignore the desperate pleas echoing inside me, "Let me out! Let me out!"

Believing God's Word held the key to my escape, I parked my mind on every "fear not" verse I could find. I memorized some, but mostly I journaled new verses every day that promised the same thing—freedom. I held my thoughts captive to this one idea that my Instructor repeated often—*Perfect love casts out fear.* Some mornings my lips uttered words from Mark's gospel, "Be not afraid, just believe," before my fingers reached the snooze button on the alarm.

As the sun lifted itself above the horizon every dawn, so my aspiration strained toward the noonday sun. The more I drew near to God, the more my Creator drew near to me. God's passion for my release grew clearer with every promising story and verse, showered upon me morning after morning. Then one day, like a gift carefully considered and thoughtfully wrapped, God graciously showed me a vivid image of my fear. Understanding erupted like a rainbow after a sun-shower.

My fear looked like a rude fat man living in my basement—much like an insensitive houseguest who'd overstayed his welcome. Imposing himself in a corner of my lower level, his hideout was black, shiny, and round with walls constructed of kryptonite.

The grumpy guy wore a black robe, corded around his rotund belly. Reclining on a torn couch, he excelled at overeating and tossing garbage on the floor. His desire for food was insatiable and he fed on my fear—thus his obesity. If I would just stop feeding him, he would not exist.

I tried telling him to leave, but he yelled at me. His loud voice scared me, sending me skittering away from the door. I stood in the hallway cowering, fretting, and wondering what to do. I felt stuck. Stuck in the basement with an arrogant food fanatic.

That's when Jesus walked in. He entered the shiny door without knocking. He yelled at the fat man. "You have no business in this house and you cannot live here anymore. GO!" Then He grabbed him by the collar and threw him out. As He walked toward me, His arms outstretched for a hug, the misplaced house disappeared and all was as it should be.

Without question, kowtowing to the crabby overeater paled in comparison to hugging Jesus. So empowered was I by the idea that my fear resembled an undesirable tenant that I grew less and less tolerant of its antics.

Drawn in to Scripture, my heart pounded one morning as my eyes fell upon words from Isaiah 22. I read "This is what the Lord, the Lord Almighty, says: 'Go, say to this steward, to Shebna, who is in charge of the palace: What are you doing here and who gave you permission to cut out a grave for yourself here, hewing your grave on the height and chiseling your resting place in the rock? Beware, the Lord is about to take firm hold of you and hurl you away, O you mighty man. He will roll you up tightly like a ball and throw you into a large country. There you will die and there your splendid chariots will remain—you disgrace to your master's house! I will depose you from your office, and you will be ousted from your position.'"[7]

Greatly encouraged, I wrote in my journal a few days later, *In my heart God is pouring water on the dry ground. I feel it. Maybe it is just a trickle now, but I feel the dam is about to break and let out a bold, unafraid, laughing, overflowing river within me. I am excited with anticipation. It seems too good to be true, but it is.*

A couple days later, Isaiah's words reassured me again: "The cowering prisoners will soon be set free; they will not die in their dungeon, nor will they lack bread."[8]

Exhilarated with expectation by God's persistent loving attention to me and my problem, I pondered those verses, rested on God's strength, and agreed with God's agenda. I didn't have to fight—I knew Jesus would. With holy fear, I just believed.

Eleven days after the journal entry, I stood in my living room, full of desire to worship. All alone, I cranked up the stereo and sang. Before long, unintended laughter burst forth and tears poured down my cheeks. A wonderful feeling of release commenced, though I did not understand. Even so, I launched into the day's activities with an added bounce in my step.

Hope's delight dawned with the next day's sunrise. When friends stopped by unexpectedly for a visit, I marveled at the freedom with which I spoke words I'd long withheld. As the midday sun ambled toward the western horizon, creaky house noises and temperamental pipes no longer put me on edge. The fruit of hope had proven true, and I couldn't contain the parade inside myself. Free, at last, to be me, I stepped outside and reveled in the heaven-sent breeze caressing my cheek. My spirit was no longer slave to the overbearing demands of a gluttonous thief. Fear had packed its bags and left.

I believe Isaiah was right—there is a day of reckoning in the valley of vision—a day of tumult and trampling and terror, a day of battering down walls. A day when praise may bring the answer to a simple prayer. A day of understanding that when God says, "Fear not," God intends to hold your hand and help you do it. And when that happens, you know the day of putting dungeon dwellers on notice has arrived, and you discover anew the deep, deep love of Jesus.

---

*This experience in Brenda's life remains a milestone in her faith walk. She has discovered that living free is a lot more fun. Prone to risk-taking these days, she's even been sighted standing dangerously close to the edge of her bed.*

## A Quarrel Not My Own
### By Jean Swenson

"Jean, could you do me a favor?" A close friend had called to update me on her difficult situation. I listened in sympathy.

"The divorce is going through," she continued, "and the court hearing is coming up. You know my husband and our situation. Could you write a letter stating your honest observations of his behaviors over the past few years?"

I hesitated. I *could* write such a letter, but *should* I? "May I pray about this and get back to you?"

"Sure," she answered. "But could you possibly let me know by tomorrow, as my attorney is in the process of putting everything together?"

"Oh Lord," I sighed as I hung up the phone. "I really need your wisdom on this."

Wisdom—the ability to see this situation from God's perspective and do what was best—yes, that was exactly what I needed. I really wanted to support my friend, and she wasn't asking me to do anything unethical. In truth I'd seen things that would strengthen her case, but something made me feel uncomfortable with her request.

As I prayed about it that evening, a Scripture came to my mind, complete with the image of a person grabbing a growling dog by the ears. I looked it up in my concordance and found Proverbs 26:17: "He who meddles in a *quarrel not his own* is like one who takes a passing dog by the ears." Ouch! Was God using a picturesque verse in Proverbs to warn me against getting involved in this particular quarrel?

I'd read that verse many times. In fact, I've been reading through the thirty-one chapters of the book of Proverbs for years. I read a chapter each day—chapter one on the first day of each month, chapter two on the second, and so on. I've read through Proverbs so many times that I know numerous portions by heart, benefiting from King Solomon's timeless wisdom that focuses on such everyday issues as building healthy relationships, handling finances, maintaining emotional and physical health, discerning the character of others, and preparing children for successful living.

For example, Proverbs reveals the importance of our words as we relate to others: "There is one whose rash words are like sword thrusts, but the tongue of the wise brings healing. . . . The mind of the righteous ponders how to answer, but the mouth of the wicked pours out evil things. . . . Death and life are in the power of the tongue, and those who love it will eat its fruits." How often the following axiom has kept me out of trouble: "Even a fool who keeps silent is considered wise; when he closes his lips, he is deemed intelligent."[9]

My thoughts returned to my friend and her request. Although she admitted that her responses weren't always perfect, her husband's selfish and foolish choices were inflicting excruciating pain and hardship on her and their children. (He obviously was not reading his daily chapter of Proverbs!)

What to do? I didn't want to base this important decision on a general principle that may not apply to every situation, and I knew that wrong decisions and false doctrines were often supported by applying Scripture out of context. After all, there were countless other Scripture verses whose general principles could justify writing that letter, such as Proverbs 3:27:

"Do not withhold good from those who deserve it, when it is in your power to act."

*Okay, God,* I prayed, *I'm leaning toward not writing that letter and I'm not sure why, because I do want to support her. But you know things about this situation that I don't. Please help me know beyond a doubt what you want me to do.*

The next morning I began reading my regularly scheduled chapter in Proverbs 25. When I reached verse eight, I stopped.

"What you have seen with your eyes, do not bring hastily to court, for what will you do in the end if your neighbor puts you to shame?"

I reread that verse and felt a deep sense of peace. *Don't write the letter,* God seemed to be telling me directly that morning. Was I only looking for something that would back up my initial hesitation? No, other verses hadn't grabbed my attention, not like this or like the one about quarreling dogs. I paused for a moment, waiting to see if God would direct me to look elsewhere or guide me in another way. But the sense of peace only grew stronger.

"Thank you, Lord," I prayed out loud. "Thank you for directing me in this decision. Thank you that your Word is so practical and alive."

How would I tell my friend, though? Often, what one person views as obedience to God is interpreted by someone else as being uncaring. God had clearly guided me, but would she understand? Every time I considered picking up the phone to call her, fears of how the conversation might go made me put it off.

Later that day, she called again.

"Well, Jean," she said, "have you made your decision?"

"Uh, well, yes," I answered. "I prayed about it, and, well, I'm just not getting a green light to write that letter."

"Okay," she said. "I just needed to know. Let me know if you change your mind."

My tension melted away. She'd simply accepted my decision. "I'll continue to pray for you and your situation," I said, relieved and grateful. "Please keep me posted."

"Thanks, I could definitely use your prayers."

"Lord," I immediately prayed after hanging up, "please guide my friend through this difficult time. Keep me faithful to support her through prayer and encouragement. And thank you for guiding me so clearly through your Word."

Who would have thought that a couple of obscure Bible verses, penned nearly three thousand years ago, could guide me so clearly in so perplexing a decision!

---

*Jean loves reading her "chapter a day," continually amazed at how often this ancient wisdom is exactly what she needs as she navigates through her days. She still prays for her friend, who is trying to pursue God in the midst of very difficult circumstances.*

## A New Relationship
*Jill Samuelson-Omath*
*As told to Sharon M. Knudson*

The phone rang in our house, and the caller ID told me it was my husband, Matt. He'd gone to the post office to mail our September estimated taxes.

*What could he want? Had he been in an accident?*

"I want a divorce," he said with a sharp edge to his voice.

*What?* My thoughts and words seemed to freeze. What kind of a man calls his wife on the cell phone and says that? This couldn't be happening. He'd never hinted at separating.

"What do you mean?" I finally said. For some time I'd had a feeling something was wrong because he'd been spending countless hours locked in his office with the computer and not sleeping in our bed. Besides completely shutting me out, he had become hypercritical of everything from my cooking to the way I dressed and wore my hair.

"I had no idea you were thinking about a divorce! Can't you reconsider? Can't we go to counseling? I'll do anything . . ."

"NO!" he said. "I've met someone else and I want a divorce."

I heard the phone disconnect, but I continued to hold it to my ear. *This must be a dream,* I thought. My body started to tingle and my mind went numb.

Matt bounded through the door two hours later. He wouldn't look at me or talk to me, other than snapping, "I meant what I said."

I retreated to our bedroom, not wanting to feel his hateful stares. If he really left, what would I do? Where would I live? Our two little girls were just two and four years old. What would I tell them? I curled up, hugging my knees, trying to stop my hands from shaking. *God, help me. . . .*

At church a few Sundays before, a man had spoken about an upcoming Alpha study for people who wanted to know more about the Christian faith. Now his words came back to me. He was handsome and tall with curly hair, and instead of sounding like he had all the answers, like some Christians I'd heard, he humbly mentioned that for years he'd had problems in his marriage. "The ten weeks of Alpha helped me understand God and what I believe, really for the first time."

Could I find help in such a course? "Maybe this is just what I need," I murmured to myself.

The course start date was two weeks away. I found myself almost counting the hours. Yet the first night, the crowd was far larger than I expected. I almost walked out, but people smiled and nodded without overwhelming me. I took a seat at a back table and watched as the leaders started the discussion. They seemed warm, caring. When the evening ended, I knew I'd be back.

The next week, all of us were offered Bibles to take home if we needed one. I'd never owned a Bible. This one had a soft white cover. I opened its pages and sampled the clear, modern phrasing of the New Living Translation. Maybe I *could* get something out of its pages. Once back in my car, I gently set the Bible on the seat beside me, its white cover shining in the moonlight, stirring hope in me.

Coming through the door of our house that night yanked me back to reality, though. While my husband had continued his insults and criticisms all along, my new possession provided him with new descriptive phrases.

"So you're a Bible-banger now?" he shouted. "Jesus freak! Just remember, we have a court date for the divorce tomorrow!"

Tears filled my eyes as the happiness I'd felt at church crumbled. I rushed to the bathroom, the one place I could be alone, flinging my new white Bible toward the bed as I passed. I stayed there until my emotions were under control.

Finally, my eyes dried, I stepped out again. My Bible was lying open on the bed, right where I'd tossed it. I picked it up, being careful not to disturb the pages, and read, "I am worn out from sobbing. Every night tears drench my bed; my pillow is wet from weeping. My vision is blurred by grief; my eyes are worn out because of all my enemies. Go away, all you who do evil, for . . . the Lord has heard my plea; the Lord will answer my prayer."[10]

*God sees my pain,* I thought, *and is sorry I'm having to go through this . . .* I highlighted those verses, read them a few more times, and felt peaceful enough that I was able to drift off to sleep.

The next morning I decided to take my Bible with me to court as I directed silent prayers for composure and assistance to heaven.

Matt's lawyer saw the white Bible clutched to my chest and announced crisply, "You can't bring a Bible into the courtroom."

"I can, and I will," I replied. "This is the only thing that's going to get me through this ordeal."

So I kept my Bible out on the desk, in plain sight, the words of the psalm echoing in my thoughts and forming my prayers.

That Bible proved an inexhaustible source of comfort during the year-long battle for custody of our daughters. I highlighted any verse that was meaningful to me. I used Post-it Notes to mark passages I knew I'd want to find again. I slept with my Bible at night. Through the class, I learned that I'd never taken time to build a relationship with God. As my understanding of God grew, so did my inner calm, despite the outward turmoil of the divorce.

I don't want to minimize the pain and rejection the divorce caused me, nor suggest that I was without fault in the six years we were married. Yet, after that awful night, when God, through the Psalms, spoke to me and said, *"I understand . . . I'm here,"* I no longer felt like I was facing an uncertain future alone. God helped me keep functioning. I also felt God helping me as I spoke with my daughters about their father, keeping any resentment and anger at bay that could have tainted their relationship with him.

After the divorce was finalized, I had to return to work for financial reasons. When my old friends saw me, they asked, "What's changed about you? You look so happy!"

I'd always smile and say, "Well, let me tell you. It's about this new relationship. . . ." A relationship that I discovered with the help of my Bible when I needed it most.

*Jill is now remarried to a lifelong Christian. She and Ken have a blended family made up of Kyle and Cody, ages 13 and 11, and Madison and Cassidy, now 8 and 6. The four children all know they are children of God and really love each other. Jill says that although four years ago she was asking God, "Why is this happening to me?" she now knows that God used her troubled marriage to teach her how to love herself, others, and her Creator.*

## KEY: The Bible is still our sovereign source for discovering God's will.

Though it may be tricky to use the Bible for guidance, it isn't meant to trick us. It isn't a crystal ball. While I've heard of people receiving guidance by opening its pages and blindly pointing to a verse, remember the tale of the woman who was arrested for stealing after she took the advice of 1 Corinthians 3:21, "All things are yours."

In all seriousness, the Bible is easier to use for general guidance than for specific questions. You can find timeless wisdom concerning marriage, work, parenting, and other day-to-day concerns that often pose big dilemmas. But if you're looking for a specific answer to a specific question, note that in the above stories the writers were searching and listening for what God had to say to them. Even in the story about writing the letter, God brought the verse about fighting dogs to Jean's mind; she used several portions of Scripture and listened for what God was trying to say to her.

If you're new to using the Bible for guidance, here's how you might proceed:

- Begin by studying the Bible, either in a small group or in a class, to familiarize yourself with its themes and structures and its portrayal of God.
- Clarify what you are asking of the Bible. If you're looking for an answer to a specific question rather than general wisdom or values, other sources of guidance may be better.
- Consider what the whole Bible has to say. Remember that at the Council of Jerusalem, both sides of the circumcision question used Scripture to support their views.
- Remember that the Bible clearly tells us that some matters are disputable (Romans 14 lists Sabbath laws and dietary requirements, for example); Christians will hold different opinions on those matters, and that is okay.
- Check your interpretations with those of others. Not one of us, not even the greatest biblical scholar, will always get it right.

The more you study, the more you listen, the more you get to know your Creator, the easier using the Bible for guidance will become.

*Lord, how can I ever grasp all that your Word can tell me?*
*So much wisdom, yet*
> *difficult names*
> *strange customs*
> *complicated laws*
> *challenging commandments*
> *perplexing parables.*

*Still, your guidance runs through it all.*
*Help me learn to use its pages to draw closer to you,*
> *to understand what you would have me do. Amen.*

---

[1]Genesis 17:10
[2]Acts 10:15
[3]Matthew 5:17–18
[4]Acts 15:16–17
[5]2 Timothy 3:16–17 NRSV
[6]Isaiah 43:1
[7]Isaiah 22:15–19
[8]Isaiah 51:14
[9]These verses are from, respectively, Proverbs 12:18, 15:28, 18:21, and 17:28 RSV
[10]Psalm 6:6–9 NLT

# 4

# Can I Ever Trust My Own Heart?

Key: The gifts and talents you've been given are part of God's plan for you.

*The people of Israel wanted a king. They demanded a king, telling their judge, or spiritual leader, Samuel, "You are old, and your sons do not walk in your ways; now appoint a king to lead us, such as all the other nations have."* [1] *Samuel prayed, knowing that God alone was king of Israel, but the Lord told him to give the people a king—Saul, of the tribe of Benjamin.*

*The Bible tells us that Saul was "an impressive young man without equal among the Israelites—a head taller than any of the others."* [2] *He looked like a king. Further, as the story unfolds, Samuel could not have made it more clear to Saul that God had chosen him to be king. He anointed him with oil. He gave him the most important cut of meat at a banquet. He told him of many signs, all of which came to pass. And then, God filled Saul with the Spirit.* You are chosen of God, *the circumstances screamed. But . . .*

---

Saul sank to the ground, out of breath, then crouched lower. Still, he feared that someone would spot him amidst the piles of baggage, a poor but handy hiding place. *If only I could disappear altogether,* he wished fervently.

Sounds of the crowds swirled around him. Every able-bodied person in Israel had traveled to Mizpah to see whom Samuel would crown as king of Israel.

Saul hadn't even told his family about meeting Samuel, about being anointed. It couldn't be real. He wasn't a king but a farmer, and not a very good one at that. He couldn't even find his father's donkeys. That's how all this craziness had started, when he'd sought out Samuel the prophet to ask about those lost donkeys.

Tonight he'd sat by his father and the rest of the clan of Matri until Samuel had declared that God had chosen the king from the tribe of Benjamin. His tribe. Slowly, he'd stood up and backed away from the gathering. *If Samuel really brings me forward, everyone will laugh.*

Samuel was so old . . . that's why the people had demanded a king. Maybe he'd misunderstood God, gotten this all wrong. Why would Yahweh choose a king from the smallest tribe? And from one of the least powerful families? Besides, he knew nothing of being a king—leading armies, settling disputes, making new decrees.

A shout rose up from the crowd. Cries of, "Matri, Matri!" His clan's name. *This can't be happening.* He closed his eyes, remembering the feel of oil trickling down his neck as only the week before, Samuel had gone through the motions of anointing him. *God, before it's too late . . . show Samuel the man you've* really *chosen as king.*

"There he is—Saul!" a voice shouted. Hands grabbed his shoulders, hauled him to his feet, pushed him forward, into the presence of Samuel. By this time, Saul's heart was pounding so hard that he feared he would faint then and there.

"Come," the prophet said firmly. Saul stared at the ground, cemented to the spot. He felt a hand on his chin, tilting his face upward until he was looking into the face it belonged to . . . Samuel.

Saul searched the old man's face, looking for signs of indecision or confusion. But all he saw was kindness.

"You *are* the chosen one," the prophet said firmly. Then Samuel turned to the crowd and said, "Do you see the man the Lord has chosen? There is no one like him among all the people."

As the crowd cheered, "Long live the king!" Samuel turned to Saul and said, "Remember, the Spirit of God has made you a different person—not Saul the farmer but God's chosen king."

*King Saul . . . will I ever get used to it?* the young man pondered as the people shouted his name.

————

*Saul ruled for 42 years. At first, the leadership qualities that God had given him shined. But all too soon, Saul ignored God's directives. God withdrew His favor. Did Saul succumb to arrogance? Impatience? Or insecurity?*

*Perhaps the way Saul hid in the baggage showed his real problem. Perhaps he never really believed that he was cut out to be king; he was afraid to use the gifts and talents God gave him.*

*But those God-given talents, gifts, and passions are clues to what God wants us to do. What keeps you from developing yours? Fear of failure? Lack of self-worth? Disbelief that using them might put you exactly where God wants you to be? The following stories show how God leads us through the way we were created, helping us become all we were meant to be.*

> For you created my inmost being . . . I praise you because I am fearfully and wonderfully made; your works are wonderful, I know that full well.[3]

## Dreams of Flying
*By Bill Yon*

I glanced at my watch again, but the minute hand had barely moved. The walls of the car-rental agency I managed were closing in on me. The phone was silent; no one rented cars in Phoenix during the off-season. This was no way for me to make a living.

As I straightened the travel brochures, a picture of a plane caught my eye. I'd had so much fun earning my solo pilot's license back in high school. Why hadn't I become a pilot?

That summer I earned my commercial license and instrument rating, bought co-ownership in a Piper Apache to build up multi-engine flight hours, and worked toward flight-instructor certification to help pay my bills.

I also took an airline ground crew job at the Phoenix airport, hoping to edge into a pilot spot. One November morning I was the gate lead for a 757. With me was a new employee, just learning the ropes.

I plugged my headset into the nose gear. After eyeing things up, I spoke to the pilot, signaled to the tug driver, then looked over at the trainee to make sure she was safe.

In the split second that my head was turned, the tug driver turned the plane. The 757's wheel caught me in the ankle, slamming me to the pavement. White-hot pain shot through me as the wheel rolled up my leg. Desperate, I tried to twist away. The wheel slipped off my knee, but continued alongside my body, catching the skin under my arm before the plane finally slowed to a halt.

I tried to get up, to escape the shadow of the plane towering over me, but I couldn't move my leg. Someone pressed me gently to the tarmac. Someone else tossed his jacket over my leg and fumbled with my ID tag. "It's okay, Bill, you're all right."

My leg felt engulfed in flames, but the words helped me focus. Waiting for the ambulance and during the whole bumpy ride to the hospital, I prayed, *God, help me keep breathing . . . in . . . out . . . don't let me lose control.*

The next day the doctors asked me to wiggle my toes. I asked, "Could I see my leg?" One glance and I had to turn away from the misshapen, tangled mess. I heard myself asking, "When are you going to take it? Can you save my knee?"

The doctor sighed. "We can try, but . . ."

The damage was too great. They operated twice, finally finishing the amputation above the knee. I kept telling myself, *Just thank God that you survived being run over by a plane.* I knew amputees who lived normal lives. But could I fly again?

The airline flew Wally, my college roommate and hockey pal, down to see me. I was pretty groggy, but I joked that he'd finally be able to skate faster than me.

"Hey, just remember," Wally said, "if there were fifteen thousand things you could do before, there's still ten thousand now. Let's focus on the ten thousand."

I tried to joke, "No ice hockey, but ice fishing, ice cream . . ."

*And flying,* I hoped.

Two days after my release from the hospital, I hopped into my plane's cockpit unassisted. My buddy worked the pedals, but I managed the hand controls. As the ground dropped away, the steady drone of the plane's engine was the best music ever. I had to keep flying.

When I got my first prosthesis, I spent evenings on the edge of my bed, maneuvering my new foot and applying toe pressure to imaginary brake and rudder pedals.

The practice paid off. That spring, after a two-hour flight test, the FAA granted me a waiver of demonstrated ability. I could fly anything my licenses qualified me for.

I started giving flying lessons. I didn't want to be known as "that instructor with one leg," but word got around. Even though I wore long pants, I sensed students staring at my leg. One even asked, "How do you work the brakes?"

I joked, "Do you think I'd get into this plane if I couldn't stop it?" I worried, though, whether the airlines would have doubts about me, too. Well, I'd simply work harder than other pilot candidates.

To build flight hours, I flew back to my hometown, Roseau, Minnesota. While visiting friends, I met Tami Hedlund, a law student who'd graduated from my high school a few years behind me. We clicked right from our first date at the county fair.

With more trips home to see Tami, I quickly accumulated enough hours to apply to a major airline. The flight-simulator tests and interviews seemed to go well.

Within a few days, a letter appeared in my mailbox. Unable to wait, I tore it open as I walked up the driveway. It was a form rejection slip. I'd failed the physical because of my leg.

Back inside, I sat down and read that statement again and again. *God, could the airline be right about my disability? Could my leg fail me by acting up in the midst of a flight emergency?* It still hurt.

*You're already twenty-eight; maybe you're just chasing dreams,* I told myself. I couldn't ask Tami to marry me until I had a solid career. Wouldn't choosing a more realistic path be the mature thing to do?

That was it; I quit flying and took a management position in the aerospace program at the University of North Dakota. Tami and I married just a year after we met.

But I couldn't stop thinking about flying. At work, I sat at a desk and handed pilots their flight schedules. Worse, airlines were hiring again. Almost weekly, one of my pilots resigned, announcing who he or she'd be flying for. I kept thinking, *You pilots had better love it as much as I did.* Once again I was stuck in an office, wondering what else I could do.

This time I combined my hockey experience and business degree to pursue a retail sporting goods store. For a year I immersed myself in the details—choosing a location, selecting merchandise, and procuring funding.

It all fell apart at the last minute. That night I couldn't sleep for thinking of the effort I'd wasted. In the morning I told Tami, "If I'd put that time into flying, I'd know by now whether I could have made it to the airlines."

Tami looked at me. "The airlines might still let you fly? I thought not being a pilot was a given. We never talked about it."

I explained why I'd quit. "Now I'm wondering if God wanted me to or if I was merely too afraid to try."

"If you still want to fly so badly, maybe it's what God has in mind for you. After all, God wants the best for you. Go for it. No more living with *What if*s."

That summer I scheduled myself to pilot several charter flights, gradually building up hours. Then in August, an old pilot friend of mine called. He said, "I'm flying the company plane these days and I'm short a copilot tomorrow. Any chance you can join me?"

Could I! The day dawned crystal clear. We were only headed to southern Minnesota, but being in the cockpit of a full 19-passenger plane made me feel like a real pilot. I reached for the copilot checklist, but my friend said, "No, you're flying this thing today."

For an instant I wondered about my prosthesis. Could it hinder me in flying big planes? My heart started pounding. *Come on, Bill, this is just a plane, like all the others you've flown*. I concentrated on the feel of the controls in my hands, the sights out the windows. The hammering in my chest eased as we leveled off.

Coming into Austin, Minnesota, there was a significant left-to-right crosswind. To land smoothly, I'd have to "feel" my prosthesis, give just the right amount of toe pressure to the pedals. Nervously I told myself, *If you can land this, you can land anything. Just concentrate*. I applied right-rudder pressure to straighten the plane's nose, lowering the wing a bit to adjust for the wind. The plane bounced ever so slightly, then taxied to a smooth stop. The pilot said, "Nice job."

I executed two more landings on our way home. As soon as we refueled the plane and pushed it back into the hanger, I called Tami on my cell phone. "Honey, I actually got to fly—even made the landings."

"Hey, that's great!" Tami sounded as excited as me.

I recounted every takeoff and landing. "I'm going for it. Thank God I had the courage to try flying again."

Five months later, I sat in the cockpit of an even larger plane, wearing a Mesaba Airlines pilot's uniform. Lucky there wasn't a mirror or I might have stared at my real pilot's hat rather than the controls. As I made my first official landing approach, I checked the readings one more time, then maneuvered the pedals automatically. The wheels eased onto the runway as smoothly as if I'd done it a million times.

Climbing out of my seat, I bumped my right leg against the instrument panel. In the excitement of the flight, I'd forgotten all about my prosthesis. Perhaps waiting on my dream for almost a decade gave me time to get comfortable with my ability to handle a plane as an amputee—and to learn that my dreams and God's dreams for me can be one and the same.

————————

*After four years of living his dream with the airlines, Bill decided that he wanted to be home more to spend time with his two children. He took a pharmaceutical sales job and has been enjoying this new challenge. He misses flying very much but is extremely grateful that he was able to achieve his goal of being a pilot.*

## Buried Treasure
*By Carol Oyanagi*

My manager's words stung me. We sat in the break room, surrounded by stacks of shrink-wrapped software packages.

"Since you're not serious about software sales, we're changing your status to part time."

*Not fair,* my heart cried. I couldn't afford to reduce my hours. But I also felt betrayed. I'd taken the sales job on the promise that it could evolve into a training position. I'd been a technical writer and thought training might allow me to use more of my creative skills. But the position had remained straight sales, so I'd finally told my manager I'd be pursuing another job, giving him time to find a replacement. Was this my reward?

"Lord, I need a new job," I prayed.

Within a few days, a woman from a placement agency called about an administrative position at an architectural firm.

"From your résumé, I see you've had a lot of word-processing experience," she said. I knew several software packages and typed at a reasonable speed, but I didn't enjoy that kind of work. Still, I didn't have many other options.

The interview took place in an artistically designed conference room. I sat at a polished wood table with the human resources manager and one of the partners. "It's a great environment," they eagerly told me, "with many opportunities for growth."

*Maybe I can make this better,* I told myself. I gathered some courage and asked, "Could my duties expand to include software training?"

"That'd be helpful," the human resources manager said, "especially word processing and spreadsheets."

"And . . . I have a writing degree. Have you considered an in-house newsletter?"

"Excellent!" they replied.

The whole situation had a happily-ever-after feel, other than the emphasis on word processing. I knew from experience how it drained my creativity. Still, the training and newsletter design would add variety.

Any remaining doubts disappeared when the placement agency representative called. "They raved about your skills," she said. "They even used the word *love.*" My heart melted. Of course I'd take the job. God had swung open a door for me and my talents would be well received.

I started in June. Dressed in a new green suit, I sat down at my computer and plunged in with little training or instruction. Within a few hours, the demands of the work fell on my shoulders and tied them into knots. Inundated with projects from five different architects, I found myself updating fifty-page technical specifications and reformatting charts that ran for ten or more pages.

Though my fingers flew across the keyboard, my sixty-words-per-minute typing rate was no match for the previous administrative assistant's eighty. Locating files took forever, too, because of a numbering system no one explained to me.

Near the end of the day, a shadow fell across my desk. When I turned, one of the architects stood behind me, literally looking over my shoulder.

"I'm just trying to encourage you to work faster," he said.

I clamped my mouth shut and turned back to my computer, doing my best to ignore him. He continued to lurk until the completed document rested in his hands.

By September I hated my job—and it seemed to hate me in return.

With so much rapid typing, my wrists and fingers experienced numbness and shooting pains. I also developed a rash all over my body and often felt nauseated after sitting for long hours at my desk. *God, if you want me here, why are all these bad things happening?* I wondered.

Small solutions came. I spent one Saturday streamlining the filing system. I also went to a dermatologist, took frequent breaks to ease the strain of typing, and started exercising. Eventually the lurking architect left me alone and trusted me to complete his work.

Though my health and typing speed improved, in December I asked God for a way out. I was frustrated, yet I didn't want to give up. Longing to work on all the creative projects I had initially proposed, I doggedly kept at my work, telling myself, *If I complete my daily assignments faster, I'll have a little extra time to develop a newsletter or plan software classes.*

Eventually I held one small training session, but only because I had prepared the materials on my own time. I obtained approval for the name and logo design of the in-house newsletter, but that was as far as I got.

On January 1, I made my annual New Year's resolutions. I still hated my job, but I decided to accept it for what it was. Even if I didn't get to use my talents, I needed to be content unless God wanted me to do something different.

Three days later I was called into the conference room. When I saw the vice-president and the former "lurker" sitting at the polished wood table, I sank into my chair.

"Our firm is not doing as well as we hoped," the vice-president began. "We're going to have to let you go."

Several employees, including myself, were being laid off. Tears formed in my eyes. The attractive artwork on the walls blurred into a finger-painted mess.

"It's not about you or your work," said the architect. "The economy's tight, and a lot of businesses are struggling."

I returned to my desk and blindly gathered my wits along with my personal items. If God had truly opened a door for this job, why did I now feel sweet relief that it was closed? Looking around the office for the last time, why did I feel okay about saying good-bye to the tedious typing, the wrist pains, and the sickness? God wanted me to *enjoy* my work. Somewhere another job existed, more suitable for how God had created me. It was out there, like a hidden jewel, but I knew I'd have to search for it.

Before I left I said good-bye to the human resources manager.

"I'm sorry we didn't get to use your skills," she said, her eyes cast downward.

"That's all right. I'm sure there's probably something better for me," I said. "It's not like I'll be searching for another job. I'll be hunting for buried treasure."

She smiled and hugged me.

A string of less-than-perfect jobs followed before I finally focused on my own writing. When my first newspaper article was published five years later, I felt God saying, *"For this you were created."*

But what about the other jobs I had? Were they a waste of time? I soon realized that each non-creative position gave me skills I needed to manage a writing career. My technical-writing background taught me how to research. Marketing my work, I use skills I developed when I sold software. My business records and tracking systems look very similar to what I used at the architectural firm. And, after those painful layoffs, a rejection letter from a publisher is no excuse to give up.

God took each of my experiences—good and bad—and turned them into learning tools. Now if I see a door, I think a little harder about whether it's open or closed. After all, it isn't easy to open doors in the world of writing, and closed doors don't always stay that way. If I think I'll enjoy the work, and if I can use the talents I've been given, I'll walk through the door or wait for it to open, knowing my path will continue to lead me toward God's treasures.

———

*After searching for buried treasure on many different paths, Carol now enjoys "the toughest job she's ever loved"—pursuing projects in writing and dance. Often working more than full time, she no longer deals with wrist pains, rashes, or nausea. She uses her training skills to teach dance to children and adults, her desktop-publishing skills to choreograph, her writing and sales skills to prepare marketing pieces, and her organizational skills to keep accurate business records. Though she hasn't found homes for her book-length projects yet, she knows not to give up and is thrilled watching God use her daily experiences in her writing.*

## A Lifetime of Purpose
*By Joanne M. Tarman*

"Shut up!" five-year-old Laura blurted as she slapped my cheek. Not the greeting I'd hoped for, but I didn't care. We were finally meeting face-to-face.

I wanted to tell her, "Hi, little one. I've been praying for you for a long, long time." However, I didn't dare in front of Ellen,[4] her social worker. Ellen suspected that I was a religious fanatic who wanted to play house. She didn't seem to grasp the difference between fanaticism and *knowing* for years, at a deep level, that I would someday bring a child like Laura, with multiple disabilities, into my home.

It all started when I was a teenager. A good friend of mine, Sarah, had Down syndrome. Growing up together, we whiled away afternoons singing along to "She'll Be Comin' Round the Mountain" on her little yellow-and-white record player, or just sitting on the front steps enjoying the summer sunshine. Sarah couldn't ride a bike or play Monopoly, but her joyful spirit and tender heart made her a delightful friend. While the rest of the neighborhood kids played baseball and raced their two-wheelers, I often spent time with Sarah.

Then, when Sarah was about thirteen years old, her family moved her into a state institution. I didn't understand why, but at every opportunity I accompanied them to visit her. With each glimpse of her institutional life my heart wept. The atmosphere was stagnant and joyless, void of concern for personal dignity.

One particular summer afternoon my heart twisted as we entered the dayroom in Sarah's cottage. Rows of girls with pixie haircuts sat on straight-backed wooden chairs, rocking and moaning away their lives. As I left Sarah to an existence she loathed, God planted seeds of purpose in me that were now, many years later, finally pushing their way into the light. *Someday you'll open your home to such a child, even though you can't do more for Sarah now. . . .*

A dozen years passed, nurturing those seeds of purpose. One September afternoon my heart sensed it was time to begin the adoption process. Because I was single, two years went by before a social worker took me seriously. I changed jobs, becoming a houseparent in a group home for the developmentally disabled so I could have my daughter with me when working. As with Sarah, interacting with the adults in the group home came naturally for me.

Even so, Ellen doubted whether I was prepared. Laura had Down syndrome, just like Sarah. At age five, she still didn't walk. Ellen warned, "Laura won't always be little and cute. Adoption is forever. You can't return the child when her never-ending needs wear you out." I wanted to blurt back, "My desire to adopt is real, too, and it's God-given," but I knew Ellen would block the adoption if I insisted that God was telling me to do this. Instead, I emphasized my experience with disabled adults and how that occupation would allow me to meet Laura's needs.

On that first visit to her foster home, I watched Laura, dressed in pink corduroy pants and a flowered top, busily investigate tote bags and purses. After emptying them all, she sat quietly on the floor, watching me with her deep, dark eyes. Then, without hesitation, she crawled across the room, stretched out her arms to me, and said, "Upt." As I lifted her to my lap, God seemed to speak, *"This is the one for whom you will make my love real."* Nestling down in my arms, she brought her palm to her mouth and gently stroked her nose with her thumb—her own variation on thumb sucking.

A moment of silence—then someone said, "She seems to know." She smelled so sweet and soft. My heart ached to call her Daughter.

Laura's foster mom told me, "She only weighed three pounds at birth; heart problems, you know. She couldn't even hold her head up on her first birthday—she weighed just eight pounds." Her speech was unintelligible to those who didn't know her (except for a very clear "Shut up!"), and she was not toilet trained. I soon found out that she didn't feed herself, either. But as I watched her I thought, *Laura has more potential than she is showing*.

We progressed from visits to Laura spending full days with me, then overnights. Finally, January 12, Laura moved in with me for a six-month trial period. If all went well, I would become her mother. Jan, my adoption worker, and Ellen joined me at the foster home that morning. Amidst hugs and tears from her foster family, I promised to keep in touch. Then I carried Laura out to the car, buckled her in, and drove off to our new life together.

Those months were filled with "firsts"—pleasant firsts like shopping, eating out, and Laura's first amusement park ride. Securing her on a toddler carousel, I wondered how she would react. She clutched the wooden handles and giggled as I backed away. With a sudden jerk the carousel began moving. Startled, Laura gasped, then chuckled, then broke out in delighted laughter, riding around and around.

Other "firsts" weren't so pleasant, like doctors' appointments, stomach flu, and, worst of all, getting Laura to feed herself. She insisted on being spoon-fed. I refused. As the battle raged, I had to chuckle—I hadn't thought of my stubborn streak as a strength before.

But oh, how I needed it to help Laura become more self-sufficient. I held the spoon in her hand to "help" her feed herself. She spit out every bite. I bribed, "Eat your green beans, your favorite, and you can have a big glass of orange juice." She shook her head.

I announced, "The Muppets are on, your favorite show!" turning up the TV volume so she could hear the theme song from the kitchen. "Hurry and finish your dinner." Guess who else had a will of iron? We were a perfect match!

After a hospital stay when she'd barely eaten at all, I decided to pretend the war was over. "Laura, lunch is ready. Look, green beans!" I said, turning away. I glanced back, holding my breath. Picking up her fork, she dug in to her vegetables. The battle was over. In her mind, it seemed, she had won her victory in the hospital. *Thank you, God!*

Slowly she learned to put on her own shoes, scramble down the hall on all fours, and return wearing her jacket. By April she was daytime toilet trained. In June, she took her first steps in pursuit of a potato chip.

During the trial placement, I thought back over my long five-year struggle to adopt. I got out my calendar. Laura was born during that September when I'd clearly sensed it was time to begin actively pursuing adoption. That was no coincidence.

July found us sitting in a James County courtroom. I tried to look calm as I watched the judge flip through his thick file. Laura could still be taken away. Surely, though, the social workers had seen her thrive under my care. I wrapped my arms tightly around her and begged, *Lord, please . . .*

Finally the judge called me forward. I left Laura with Jan and stepped up into what was literally the witness stand—no chair. Feeling unsteady, I grasped the waist-high railing that surrounded the wooden box on three sides, then turned to face the judge.

"I was very concerned about how Laura would handle this transition," he said. "I've requested frequent updates." My mouth grew dry.

He continued, "Obviously, she's very happy and has made a lot of progress. The information here confirms that. You and Laura clearly have a mutually beneficial relationship." I realized I'd been holding my breath.

Next came questions all prospective adoptive parents are asked: "Are you prepared to take on total parental responsibility for this child for a lifetime?" I had made that commitment eight months earlier.

Suddenly, the judge stopped talking and looked past me, smiling. I turned around. Laura had climbed down from Jan's lap and was toddling across the courtroom toward me with arms outstretched and palms up, her hands pulsing open and closed as she called out, "Mommy, Mommy."

I looked back at the judge. He nodded, "You may go to her." Quickly stepping down, I scooped Laura into my arms. *Thank you, Lord!* Jan was the only one present who had ever seen Laura walk. Everyone, including the skeptical social worker, smiled as they wiped away joyful tears. The judge declared official what Laura and I already knew in our hearts: We belonged to each other.

Twenty-two years later, I remember these events daily when I gaze at the doll I've dressed in the little pink corduroys and flowered top Laura wore the day I met her. Every night as I tuck my daughter in bed, I search for words to describe my joy and amazement that my God-given passion to help a child like Sarah grew into concrete love for Laura.

---

*Laura is now twenty-eight and, although stomach problems confine her to a hospital bed in the living room much of the time, she is still full of joy as she strums her electronic guitar and works on simple needlepoint mats that she is proud to give away. Joanne says, "She still delights in calling, 'Mom, I've got a secret,' and then whispering in her mother's ear, 'It's summer!' or 'I like pizza!'"*

*Laura also loves their new collie, Tessa. Joanne hopes that Tessa can be trained as a therapy dog, as she already delighted folks in wheelchairs when the three of them visited Joanne's mother in a care center as she recovered from surgery.*

## KEY: The gifts and talents you've been given are part of God's plan for you.

*I praise you because I am fearfully and wonderfully made; your works are wonderful.*[5] Do you believe that God created you with a wonderful blend of gifts and talents?

*For we are God's workmanship, created in Christ Jesus to do good works, which God prepared in advance for us to do.*[6] Do you believe that there are tasks God needs done that require your special blend of gifts? Tasks that match who you are at your very core, that excite you, that will bring fulfillment?

Or, like Saul, are you hiding in the baggage?

If you are, think for a moment about the image you carry of God. Do you picture your Creator as someone who would tell a child, "I know you're over six feet tall and can shoot ninety-five percent from the free-throw line, but you need to be a gymnast." Or, "Yes, you excel at comforting people during crises, but you have to use that time to study options and make recommendations on the next organization the church should support." No, God wants us to serve in places that match our gifts and passions, where we can flourish, where we find joy. Then we can be truly effective servants.

*En theos,* the Greek words that form the root of *enthusiasm,* mean "with God." What are you called to do that will fill you with enthusiasm, drawing you closer to God as you move forward? That path to fulfillment may not be safe or easy, but those who take it find themselves saying, "Yes, Lord! No matter what happens, for this I was created."

*Lord, help me understand the beauty of how you created me,*
    *for only then can I truly search for the good works you prepared*
    *for me.*
*Walk with me until I can say with sincerity,*
    *God loves me*
    *At my very core is the image of God*
    *God chose a special blend of gifts, personality, and passions*
    *just for me*
    *Using those gifts for God's purposes is my pathway to joy. Amen.*

---

[1] 1 Samuel 8:5
[2] 1 Samuel 9:2
[3] Psalm 139:13–14
[4] All names except for Joanne's and Laura's and the court location have been changed.
[5] Psalm 139:14
[6] Ephesians 2:10

# 5
# Was That God or Just a Dream?

**Key: Test signs against Scripture and circumstances, yet trust that God may be drawing you closer.**

*The ruling powers in Jerusalem didn't know what to do with the followers of Jesus. They arrested Peter and John, brought them before the Sanhedrin, and set them free. Then they arrested all of the apostles, but an angel of the Lord led them from jail. When they were brought before the Sanhedrin yet again, Gamaliel, one of the most honored rabbis of his time, said, "Leave these men alone! Let them go! For if their purpose or activity is of human origin, it will fail. But if it is from God, you will not be able to stop these men; you will only find yourselves fighting against God." [1]*

*Yet one of Gamaliel's students, Saul of Tarsus, spurned this advice. He watched with approval when Stephen was stoned to death. He went house to house, dragging men and women of "The Way," as the church was called at that time, off to prison. He got papers from the high priest to carry out the same mission elsewhere, in Damascus.*

*Reports of Saul's zealous persecution of people of The Way spread quickly. The people of Damascus were forewarned of this enemy. . . .*

---

Half a jar of water left. Ananias carefully poured a few drops into a cup, took a small sip, and swirled it around to moisten his parched lips. Surely someone could slip out to the well—but no. Too many people in Damascus knew that he and his household had joined The Way.

He slammed his cup down on the table. "And we won't stop talking about Jesus," he said sharply. His words sounded feeble in the shuttered house. Shaking his head, he sank down on a stool and rested his head in his hands. *God, it isn't that I'm afraid,* he prayed. *I knew that following Jesus could mean death. But is this the time? So soon?*

Only two, perhaps three, Sabbaths had passed since members of The Way from Jerusalem had sought refuge with them in Damascus. "We had to flee—they're dragging believers from their homes. Women too," they reported. "Ever since Stephen's death."

But now Damascus wasn't safe, either. Saul of Tarsus . . . "A Pharisee," the disciples from Jerusalem reported, "the most self-righteous of the bunch. He thinks he knows the Law better than his own teacher, Gamaleil."

"What?" Ananias sputtered. Gamaleil was the most revered teacher in Jerusalem.

The disciple from Jerusalem recounted Gamaleil's advice to the Sanhedrin. "He pointed out that if we weren't led by God, the movement would eventually die, like all the others started by false messiahs.

"But waiting didn't sit well with Saul. He stood as a witness to Stephen's stoning. Since then, he's gone house to house in Jerusalem, hunting us down. And now he's got letters from the high priest to do the same here, in Damascus."

So they'd gone into hiding. No sense letting Saul stumble on to one of their gatherings and arrest them all at once. "We're still in Damascus, at least," Ananias muttered, defending his actions to the empty room.

*But is this where you want us, Lord? Hidden away?*

Maybe God *wanted* him imprisoned. An angel in the night had released the apostles from the Jerusalem jail. How many new disciples joined The Way when that news got around? And Stephen—at his trial he took on the whole Sanhedrin. Maybe he'd softened a few hearts, influenced someone to change. *Lord, would I testify like that?*

He stared into his cup, now empty. Stay hidden or step out and take on Saul so that others might see the strength Jesus gave them? But what if others came to harm? If Saul arrested him, they'd come after his neighbors next . . . the young family next door with two tiny girls, the older couple who'd just seen their first grandchild. Who else would he endanger?

"Ananias!"

He started, then looked about. Was Saul outside his door even now? Carefully, he stood up. *I'll climb to the roof, escape over the housetops.* But as he moved toward the steep stairway, the air in front of him started to shimmer.

"Ananias . . ."

He squeezed his eyes shut and shook his head. What was happening? As he watched, the flickering air sifted, sparkled, shaped itself into a shadowy presence, somehow both fearsome and comforting. Could it be?

"Yes, Lord?" Ananias heard himself say, even as he sank to his knees.

"Go to the house of Judas on Straight Street."

*That's the main market,* Ananias thought. *Okay, I'm not supposed to hide anymore.*

"Ask for a man from Tarsus named Saul. He is praying there. I gave him a vision of you placing your hands on him and restoring his sight."

Ananias felt his stomach tighten, his mouth suddenly go even drier. Was this a test? "Lord, reports of how this man has harmed your saints in Jerusalem have reached us. He's here with the authority of the chief priest to do the same to us!"

Now the figure took on a different glow. Peace, a deep calm washed over Ananias, as if God was wrapping him with love.

"Go!" the Lord continued. "Saul is my chosen instrument to carry my name before the Gentiles and their kings and before the people of Israel."

Ananias gazed in wonder as the figure held up a hand as if in greeting, then slowly faded. Again he was staring at the plain walls of his home. But the warmth lingered on.

"That *was* from God," he murmured, tears springing to his eyes. "It must be true . . . but Saul? God's instrument?"

He leaped to his feet, grabbed his cloak, and hurried out the door. If God had changed Saul's heart, he couldn't wait to play his small role in this turn of events.

————

*Not only did Ananias hurry to the house of Judas and place his hands on Saul, but he called him "Brother Saul," showing his complete acceptance of what God had told him. Perhaps God needed to ensure that Ananias was confident in that acceptance. While the Bible doesn't say,*

*Ananias may have had one other task, that of convincing the other believers in Damascus that Saul's reversal wasn't part of the plot to destroy them, but a genuine conversion.*

*As the following stories show, God still guides us through prophecies, dreams, and visions. In the Bible, though, these unmistakable leadings happen at crucial moments—in the life of the church or the individual—and not for common decisions we can make based on Scripture or other sources of God's wisdom. As you read, ask yourself,* Am I ready to say yes to God?

> He calls his own sheep by name and leads them out. When he has brought out all his own, he goes on ahead of them, and his sheep follow him because they know his voice.[2]

## Mission to Mission
*By Delores Topliff*

I taped the large box shut, marveling at the generosity of the children I taught, and stood back in satisfaction. Our class project had turned out well.

Thinking of how it started still made me smile. Two months before, I'd been grading papers one afternoon in our missionary school in northern Canada, when our ham radioman rushed in: "Hurry. People in South America want to talk to you."

"To me?" Soon I was shocked but delighted to hear the voices of girls whose parents I'd trained with at a Texas missions' school. Now missionaries in Colombia, the Rankin family served the remote Caquetá region bordering Ecuador and Peru, ravaged by decades of fighting between the Army and guerrillas.

"Jungle to North Pole," their young voices said.

"Shannon, April, is that you?"

"Yes. How're y'all?"

"Fine. How are *you*?"

"Super, except they needed teachers here, and we're it!"

"Wow. You're barely through school yourselves."

"Right," they giggled, "that's why we need your help."

Love poured through the radio. The girls described how few adults in the area had ever gone to school; most of those hadn't even reached fourth grade. The mission stations were creating K–8 schools, hoping to eventually train some of the students to teach others and be part of Colombia's future. "We have nothing," they concluded. "If you could send a basic algebra text, English grammar, and biology, we'd be so grateful. . . ."

"Is that all?"

Almost hesitantly, Shannon replied that their students had never received letters. They knew little of the outside world. If my kids wrote, they'd answer.

So my class wrote thick letters telling about themselves, wild animals, the frozen North. The children's families filled the big donation box I placed in our school with books, colored pens and pencils, watercolors, stencils, math sets, stickers, and more. As I taped that box, our project seemed complete.

Eight weeks later we received their thick letters and drawings, including one from nineteen-year-old Carmen, thrilled to be in second grade, reading and writing for the first time. My students joyfully wrote back. *A nice end to a great effort,* I thought.

But that November night I dreamed it was Christmas. A relative was writing me her usual $25 gift check, only she kept adding zeroes until it read $2,500. I caught my breath, eyes wide. "THANK you," I heard myself say, "I'll use this to go to Colombia to help friends in a mission school for three to six months."

The dream seemed so real. Maybe a check *was* in the mail. Or an inheritance. But . . . I was already on a mission, in Canada. What could God possibly want me to do in Colombia?

The next morning I described the dream to my friend Esther. "I can't go—I teach almost everything at our little high school, besides being principal—and I only have thirty dollars," I confided.

"I hope it happens," she replied. "You've done wonders here. The same teaching and organizing skills apply, don't they?"

"I suppose so."

"Then let's see what God does."

Esther left, but God instantly challenged me, *"Don't depend on earthly inheritance. What if I want you to go? What if you are part of the answer to starting those schools?"*

*Me, part of the answer?* My head reeled.

For weeks I prayed, trying to discern why God might want me to go to Colombia. I *could* train teachers and write curriculum. But even if funds came, how could I leave Canada? Did that dream really come from God or was my imagination just working overtime in the excitement of hearing from Shannon and April?

"God," I prayed, "if you think my spending several months in Colombia can bless their school, I trust you to make it happen."

I shared my dream and prayers in our next church leaders' meeting. One pastor who'd made that exact trip from northern Canada to the jungle told me the cost was exactly $2,500, just like my dream. I got chills.

"They do need help," he added. "You could train teachers, among other things." His words echoed my own dawning realization that they might need my specific skills.

"Our mission fund will give one hundred dollars," our treasurer said. "More later, if we have it. Let's share this with our people and see what God does."

Responses came from the parents of kids I taught, plus other missionary teachers on shoestring budgets. One day I received three cards totaling four hundred dollars—from a co-worker, a longtime friend, and a student, all with encouraging notes saying God wanted them to be part of my trip. I sank down by the mailbox, overwhelmed, just as Esther came by.

"Stand up and praise the Lord!" she exclaimed when I showed her the checks.

"I would," I answered, "but my knees are shaking so hard, they won't hold me!"

The amount steadily grew, as did my assurance that God wanted me to go. When I had half of the money, I booked Miami-Bogotá air tickets, saving money by riding Greyhound from Canada to Florida.

When my travel date rolled around I had $2,100, still four hundred dollars short. Since God had done so much, maybe the trip would cost less. *God will provide,* I told myself, thinking back on all the assurances I'd had that I was meant to take this trip.

David, a doctor driving to a new job, took me the first leg of the journey. Our mailbox in town held another hundred.

That night we stayed with a family David knew. After dinner we talked about my trip, but I didn't mention that I was short on funds. Early the next morning the wife pressed an envelope into my hand. "I couldn't sleep," she said. "I set this aside for our kids' dental work, but God told me you need it. Herb earns overtime, so we're fine."

Inside was three hundred dollars.

A Greyhound trip. A commercial flight, then a smaller flight to Florenciá. A ride on an open bus carrying people, pigs, and chickens down a rutted road. A jungle river journey in a motorized dugout canoe. Soon I was a world away from Canada, and in Caquetá.

I joyfully greeted Shannon, April, and their parents. For the next sixteen weeks, I shared their world. Traveling up and downriver by canoe to seven mission stations, I visited schools without books, where teachers wrote lessons and drawings on blackboards for children to copy into notebooks. At each place my schedule filled with teaching students about research skills and achievement tests, training teachers, speaking to parents and churches via interpreters, and creating curriculum.

I taught in open-walled schools gorgeous with tropical hibiscus and bougainvillea vines draped in abundance. I learned to eat piranha and crocodile. I drew smiley faces on children's papers and praised teachers for their ingenuity in working with limited resources.

What had started as a dream ended in reality. Throughout my four months in Colombia, I worked on concrete tasks that were good matches for my skills—such as settling a dispute over curriculum that some leaders rightly felt was too full of Americanisms rather than the students' own rich culture.

I wanted to stay, but my visa extension was refused; the river would soon close to all traffic because of tension between the army and guerrillas. As the canoe carried me back upriver, back to Canada, I prayed for those to whom God had lead me, those I was now leaving behind.

I know that God could have found other servants far more talented than I to encourage Shannon, April, and all of the teachers up and down the river, but I will always be thankful that I knew—through the dream, through encouragement, through the prayers and generosity of those who supported me—that God wanted *me* to go!

_Since her dream led Delores on a mission trip a continent away, God has blessed her with more dreams and adventures. To date, she has completed three amazing trips through Europe and Israel. Now living in the U.S. Midwest, she stays busy teaching, speaking, and writing, but loves returning to her friends in northern Canada whenever possible. Far from finding the Christian life boring, she is a strong believer in the daily adventure of following God._

## Go!!!
_By David Stark_

As a pastor, I try to practice what I preach, literally. So nearly every morning I pull myself out of bed while it's still dark, grab my Bible, and head to my favorite chair for a conversation with God.

Usually I read a Bible passage related to something I'll be teaching soon, then try to listen for God's words to me on the topic. But one particular morning I couldn't clear my mind. To be honest, I was failing miserably with a class I was teaching.

Just a few months before, I'd taken the post of adult education minister at a new church. The women's ministry team asked me to teach a class on spiritual gifts, one of my favorite topics. I reviewed all kinds of books and course materials on the subject and chose the curriculum I thought would be best. The class was scheduled for four consecutive Wednesday mornings.

Over a hundred women signed up. It's a suburban church, filled with talented women who run everything from parent-teacher organizations to school boards to their own companies. There were probably a dozen MBAs in the room and as many attorneys or other professionals. Surely they'd learned about their gifts and talents; what would I have to add?

The first week, they'd laughed at my jokes, dug in to the study questions, and seemed to have great discussions. The second week was okay, but I felt a bit of tension. The third week, though, as they completed their spiritual gifts questionnaires, the room grew more and more silent. Silent, that is, other than deep sighs, soft coughs of disgust, and a groan here and there. I asked my table leaders to get some feedback; here's a sample of what they were told:

"I don't have any of the important gifts."

"If only I had the kinds of gifts that *she* has."

"If these are my gifts, I must have blown it. God must not trust me."

In short, eighty percent of the women concluded, "God must not love me very much if this is all I got." That was *not* what was supposed to happen, especially at a church with so many successful women.

That morning, their faces and their sorrows filled my thoughts as I tried to listen to God. Finally I stopped trying to clear my mind for prayer and instead just prayed for the class, the women, and our last session together. How could I get them to see themselves as God did?

*"Go to a bookstore."*

What? That command jolted me like a time-out buzzer at a basketball game.

*"GO TO A BOOKSTORE."*

"God, is that you?" I whispered.

*"Yes, go to a bookstore today."*

I'll be honest—for me that's a wonderful command. I love bookstores. I didn't have any early meetings, so I headed for the store nearest my home as soon as it opened. As I drove into the parking lot, a dilemma struck me. "God, I'm sure you asked me to come here, but it's an awfully big store. What am I looking for?" Silence.

I walked inside, feeling a bit sheepish as my eyes darted around the bookcases, bargain tables, and displays. I'm sure I looked lost, standing by the calendars, not sure which way to turn. Back to the religion section? Seemed probable, since God had sent me.

Then, *"Head left."* No one had spoken, but somehow I knew I was supposed to turn that direction. Magazines? Bargain books? CDs? As I walked past the business section, a tiny blue book caught my eye.

While blue *is* my favorite color, this book was minute, its spine barely a quarter of an inch across. And I was standing several feet away from the shelf it was on.

*"Look at it."*

I pulled it off the shelf. *How to Find Your Mission in Life* by Richard N. Bolles, author of *What Color is Your Parachute?* I flipped through, starting from the back, and stopped at the shaded page entitled "Some Random

Comments on Your Third Mission in Life."

> Your third Mission here on Earth is one which is uniquely yours, and that is:
> a) to exercise that Talent which you particularly came to Earth to use,
> b) in those place(s) or setting(s) which God has caused to appeal to you the most,
> c) and for those purposes which God most needs to have done in the world.[3]

As I read those words, I understood what was missing from the materials I was using: I could get the women to identify their gifts, but I couldn't get them to be *excited* about them.

*"You're going to write about this, David."* God was speaking to me again, in the middle of the business section of a bookstore! I stared at the page. It made sense. Through different activities, I could help them discover their gifts, the places for service that appealed to them, and where their gifts intersected with what God most needed done.

Still I was puzzled. *God,* I thought, *I can't write. I can preach, I can teach, but a book? No . . .*

*"Don't do it alone."*

That morning, at the class, I announced, "This is the first and last time I use these materials. I'm passing around a yellow pad for anyone to sign who wants to help me design something better!"

That was in 1992. What started with a command visit to a bookstore ended as our book *LifeKeys: Discover Who You Are.*[4] Little by little, we learned to help people discover that they are fearfully and wonderfully made, that the gifts they have were chosen by God and that God has wonderful works in mind for them to do.

Jane (the author of this book) became one of my coauthors. The third, Sandra Hirsh, whose vast experience in human resource management and training gave our process an incredible depth, turned out to be a personal friend of Richard Bolles; he graciously gave us permission to use the above quote as the structure for *LifeKeys*.

Each time we teach the class, we tell this story. You just never know what God might do if you travel to where your Creator wants you to go!

--------

*You just never know what God might do when you put your name on a yellow pad, either! I'm one of the women who took that first class, and I was the only one at my table who liked what I discovered. I came from a family where my four brothers and I were encouraged to find out how and where we could be of service, so the class confirmed what I already knew about myself.*

*When David made the announcement, I put my name on that yellow pad for two reasons. First, I was considering changing to writing full time and knew that I needed to find some concrete tasks to work on. Second, I thought that with better design and materials, we could create a class that would help people experience what my family had given me. In the whole process of creating LifeKeys, David, Sandra Hirsh, and I have felt God's guidance in so many ways.*

## God's Alarm Clock
*By Julie Chapman* [5]

I walked down the dim corridor to my room for the night, thinking how much I needed this treat of an entire evening to myself. I loved being mother to five sons, but lately the cooking, chauffeuring, laundry, and homework assistance seemed to wear me out more than usual. A weekend retreat was what I needed to recharge. Time to get photos into albums, indulge in a few catnaps, and, most importantly, pray for my mother.

Or, should I say, to pour out my anguish that despite our prayers, Mom had not been able to shake loose from the controlling, destructive grip of alcoholism. Worries over Mom had fed my recent exhaustion. I hoped that this Spartan yet contemplative setting would help me better understand how we might help her. The next day's schedule started with a 7:00 A.M. prayer service, with more opportunities for meditation and prayer throughout the day. I planned to attend all of them.

Mom was a closet drinker, in full denial that alcohol controlled her, so our attempts to convince her to seek treatment ended in ghastly arguments. It was as if our roles were reversed and she was now the child. "All you do is nag me," she'd yelled at my sister Beth and me a few days earlier. "I'm not hurting anyone but myself," Mom insisted.

"But you *are* hurting us," I wanted to scream back. That scene clarified for me that we were failing to help Mom. Maybe a full day of prayer would bring new answers.

I snapped on the light in my little room. Just a bed, a desk, a sink, and a window that looked out over a tiny courtyard. Why not start praying for Mom? The photo albums could wait. I pulled out a little book and started to read a chapter on knowing what to pray for.

As I turned a page, I caught sight of my wristwatch. It was already almost eleven. I dug into the side pocket of my suitcase to pull out my alarm clock, but it wasn't there. Frantically, I took everything out, searched through pockets and my purse, but no alarm clock.

As I changed into my nightgown I thought, *How will I wake up so early, tired as I am? Unless . . . God, will you please wake me up?* Drifting off to sleep with a prayer for Mother on my lips, I hoped God might answer my tiny request. I had really looked forward to the day-long rhythm of the services.

A steady *tap, tap, tap* roused me from a deep sleep. My room was still dark, the window barely visible in the shadows. I opened the door, but no one was there. The tapping sound seemed to be coming from the end of the corridor. I took a few steps toward the glass doors that exited outside. There, in the dim glow of dawn, stood a wild turkey, calmly but insistently pecking at the glass.

I'd never seen one before, they're still so rare in Minnesota. I glanced at my watch. It was 6:35. The exact time I would have set my alarm for to make it to the service. I laughed out loud at God's answer to my prayer. *And isn't this God's way of telling me how important it is to keep praying for Mom, even if I can't see what good it's doing?* Quickly, I dressed and brushed my hair, then hurried to the little chapel.

Throughout the day I prayed for Mom, but as the hours sped by I slowly noted that those prayers were changing from, *God, how do we fix Mom?* to *God, how do we love Mom?*

I called Beth as soon as I got home, describing the "alarm clock" God had sent for me and the focus of my prayers.

After a moment's silence, Beth whispered, "I've been worried you'd think I was nuts, but I had a . . . well . . . it was a vision of Mom's heart, dark and full of pain, like the deepest cave or dungeon you can imagine.

God told me, *'Let me direct your prayers, guide you in healing her heart.'* The image was so real."

It took me a moment to digest Beth's story. Then I said slowly, "I think God has our attention."

Those experiences, the turkey and the vision, changed how we prayed for and interacted with Mom. We called her with news. We invited her on outings. We sent cards of encouragement. We laughed together over old pictures and thanked her for the special moments she'd given us as young girls. But we stopped asking her to seek treatment.

Nearly a year passed, a year filled with doubt over whether we were doing enough for Mom. I prayed, *God, your turkey messenger affirmed my desire to keep praying no matter what, but it's so hard when nothing seems to change.*

Dad struggled more and more to pick up the pieces when Mom drank too much. One afternoon I told Mom how much I'd been praying for her. When she scoffed, I said, "God tells us to keep on praying and even helps us do it. On that retreat I told you about, I forgot to bring my alarm clock. God actually sent a wild turkey to haul me out of bed for a prayer service." A hint of a smile crossed her face when I described the bird's insistent, noisy pecking at the outside doors.

There was no magic cure. Beth called late one night. After finding Mom unconscious, she'd forced Dad to call 9-1-1. At the emergency room, a social worker arranged for Mom to be transferred to a treatment center. We'd been down this path over twenty times before, only to have her check herself out or break rules and be asked to leave. Was there any chance that this time would be different?

As soon as she could have visitors, I went to see Mom, praying as I drove, *God, will she be helped here? Let this be a good place. What should I say and do?*

I got directions to her room from the front desk and easily found the right hallway. A few pictures decorated the walls, softening the institutional surroundings. I paused before entering Mom's room to take a deep breath, close my eyes, and pray, *God, help me be loving but concerned, cheerful but serious.*

I opened my eyes, then stared at the picture outside the door of Mom's room. Autumnal oaks and maples edging a field filled with wild turkeys. A chuckle rose inside me. *"Julie,"* God seemed to say, *"I know things haven't gotten any easier, but I'm here. And I won't leave any of you."*

"Mom, did you see what's outside your door?" I said as I entered. "God sent more wild turkeys, so we'd better get praying!"

Mom smiled. I knew we were one step further along on the journey.

———

*Although the path to sobriety hasn't been smooth, Julie says that her family is communicating far better about the issues. They've grown in understanding, tolerance, and most of all in prayer. Julie's parents celebrated their fiftieth anniversary with their ten children and all of the grandchildren around them this summer. Julie and Beth continue to pray, joking that if they don't, God just may send another wild turkey!*

**KEY: Test signs against Scripture and circumstances, yet trust that God may be drawing you closer.**

Dreams. Images. Prophecies. Visits from angels. Direct commands. The Bible is filled with examples of God leading people directly in these ways. Do you believe that God still speaks to us? How would you react to a dream, a direct command, a wild turkey, if one came to you?

Go ahead and question it, as did Ananias and the writers of the stories you just read.

Check it against Scripture for consistency with the moral law of God. All too often "God told me to do it" has been used as defense for wrongful actions.

Consider asking others for interpretations. Dreams can be wishful thinking as well as guidance from God.

Keep praying and searching. Often, the guidance you get only helps you take a step or two instead of illuminating your entire way. Or, you see the end result, but it takes years to fill in the details of how to get there.

And remember, Jesus promised that the Holy Spirit would dwell within those who follow God. "But when he, the Spirit of truth, comes, he will guide you into all truth. He will not speak on his own; he will speak only what he hears, and he will tell you what is yet to come."[6] Through the Holy Spirit, God might speak directly, especially when you are about to face danger; when you need specific knowledge, as did Ananias; when God wants to change our desires or beliefs; when we need an extra measure of God's love; or when, like Saul who became Paul, we didn't listen to the first, second, or third message from God.

Take these leadings into the waiting room of your heart. Compare them to Scripture, your special design, the circumstances around you, and the wisdom of others. And above all, listen for what God might be saying.

*If you sent an angel, Lord, would I see it?*
*If you sent a dream, would I trust it in the morning?*
*Vision . . . or mirage . . .*
*Prophecy . . . or falsehood . . .*
*Command . . . or confusion . . .*
*Yet, the whisper, the directive, the leading*
*compels me, propels me forward.*
*Teach me to listen to you, and you alone. Amen.*

------------

[1]Acts 5:38–39
[2]John 10:3–4
[3]Bolles, Richard N. *How to Find Your Mission in Life*. Berkeley, CA: Ten Speed Press, 1991, p. 41.
[4]Minneapolis: Bethany House Publishers, 1996.
[5]Names have been changed.
[6]John 16:13

# 6

# How Do I Know If Something Is a Sign From God?

Key: God guides each one of us gently in ways we can best understand.

*For years, Paul had hoped to travel to Rome. He finally got the chance, but as a prisoner, headed for trial before the Emperor.*

*It was late in the sailing season. As the captain searched for a safe winter harbor, the ship got caught in a tremendous Northeaster storm that tossed and battered the ship for fourteen days and nights.*

*On the fourteenth night, as the captain and crew panicked, Paul calmly broke bread, got them to eat, and revealed that no one would die even though the ship would run aground.*

*In the morning, the ship struck rocks when they tried to steer it toward a beach. Those who could swim jumped overboard first. The rest followed, hanging on planks or other pieces of wreckage. All 276 people— crew, soldiers, prisoners, passengers—made it safely to the shores of the tiny island of Malta.*

———

Nadur brushed the raindrops from her eyes as she scanned the beach for more wood. Already she and her husband, Qrendi, had managed to coax several piles of soggy brushwood into crackling fires to warm their unexpected guests. Other villagers were doing the same.

One of the survivors approached, his arms full of driftwood. He spoke with a strange accent, but they could catch most of his words. "Thank you, we are all so tired."

"Then sit down," Qrendi said, gesturing toward the nearest fire.

The man smiled. "I need to soon."

Nadur watched him set down the wood. The other survivors parted in front of him. Was this man one of their leaders? He was dressed in a plain tunic, yet dress meant nothing when one survived a shipwreck. She caught bits of their conversation. ". . . how did you know we would survive . . ." ". . . you . . . God's favor . . ." Then the man pointed to someone, who laughed and then stood up, following to find more wood.

Qrendi was listening, too. "His name is Paul . . . someone said he speaks for God."

"If the gods favor him, why was the ship wrecked?" Nadur asked.

"They all survived. Look at where they came ashore and think—the storm surf would have pounded them against the rocks almost anywhere else."

Nadur glanced across the bay to the limestone beach where children often swam in the warm months. Its rocky ledges were only a foot above sea level, but treacherous. She'd never forget the day a wave caught her off guard as she was climbing out of the water, smashing her leg against a sharp edge. Two of the boys had to help her out. She'd limped for days. "Coming to this sandy place was lucky," she said as she stooped to pick up another piece of wood.

As they walked toward the closest fire, Paul came up with another load of wood. "Now I'll sit," he said.

He heaved the sticks onto the flames. Nadur bent to do the same, then gasped as a viper darted from the woodpile and sunk its fangs deep into the man's hand.

"Paul!" one of the other men shouted. But before anyone could reach him, the old man had calmly shaken the snake off into the fire.

One of the men pushed Paul to the ground and flung his own coat around him before examining the hand. Qrendi said, "Perhaps we spoke too soon. Maybe he is a murderer—the gods didn't want him to escape the sea. Now the snake has done their work."

Nadur shuddered. She'd tended snakebites before, watching helplessly as the affected limb swelled or the victim quickly lost consciousness, then died. "The gods are just . . ." she murmured.

By this time, other islanders had heard the commotion. "Are these strangers bad luck?" someone called out.

"What if they bring sickness?" another voiced. A crack of thunder filled the air.

Paul glanced toward them, then slowly got to his feet and walked toward Nadur. She stared into his eyes, calm and kind, as he took the wood from her arms. His hand showed no signs of swelling. Steadily, he returned to the fire and fed the wood piece by piece into the flames as they crackled in the light rain.

"Could he be . . ." Qrendi started. The villagers watched the circle of survivors for a long time as Paul handed the extra cloak back to its owner, then began telling a story about another shipwreck he'd survived. He held up a slice of bread the villagers had provided. "That time, we were adrift at sea for an entire day and night. No fires for warmth, no food. Thanks to God for this place."

Nadur concentrated on understanding the stranger's dialect. Paul spoke as if the snakebite had never happened. A woman next to Qrendi said, "He shook off the viper . . . perhaps he is a god. . . ."

*A god,* Nadur thought. *Good fortune after all.*

————

*To this day, the people of Malta celebrate the shipwreck of St. Paul that brought Christianity directly to their shores. But 2,000 years ago, people everywhere were superstitious, looking for signs from the gods in every event, good or ill. God let the natives see the incident with the snake as a sign that Paul and his people were good.*

*Those who had been shipwrecked with Paul had no way of leaving the island without a new ship. They needed the goodwill of the islanders. The people of Malta benefited as well; the Bible records that Paul performed healings in the three months he was there.*

*Can you see how the snake was just what the Maltese needed to discern what God wanted them to do: shelter and befriend Paul? Often, God seems to use signs in just this way, to give us confidence to keep moving in a direction. And the signs we get speak only to us.*

But blessed are your eyes because they see, and your ears because they hear.[1]

## About That First Date . . .
*By Jane Kise*

I leaned back in the old theater seat just as Garrison Keillor's *Prairie Home Companion* rehearsal began. It was 1980 and few people knew about the show. For four dollars, you could come an hour early, watch them practice the skits, then see the whole performance—a great deal for cash-strapped college students like us.

Tonight was typical for the friends, both men and women, that made up my college crowd; you could always find someone to go with you to the dollar midnight movie, a school dance, or events like this. After the show, we'd probably head to a little hole-in-the-wall Chinese restaurant since I was driving. Stir-fry was my absolute favorite food—and not part of our dormitory fare.

Evenings like these were simple, no strings attached, so different from dating. I shuddered, thinking of the Bruce Springsteen concert a few weeks before. I offered to pay for my own ticket rather than have the man who asked me assume it was a serious date, but he insisted on picking up the tab for the entire evening. Not even ice cream sundaes after the concert gave us much to talk about.

While some of my friends seemed to go from one serious relationship to another, I seldom dated anyone more than twice. I preferred hanging out with the gang to relationships without a future.

Still, as my senior year drew to a close, I felt a few pangs that I'd never found anyone I wanted to date more than a few times. My parents had met on this very campus; so had my eldest brother and his wife. I'd always sort of thought it would happen for me, too. *But better to stay single than marry the person you were dating your senior year of college just because of the timing,* I thought.

One November Sunday I awoke filled with guilt over the amount of cake and ice cream I'd consumed at a birthday party the night before. Even though I needed to study, I decided to head to the pool during open swimming. I'd been on the diving team for most of my college years; a swim would help me concentrate.

When I got there, I decided to goof around on the boards for a bit, put in a couple of my favorite dives. While my best showing at Division 3 nationals had been 33rd out of 66, I could still rip a few basics. Then I got down to business and swam a thousand yards. *There,* I thought to myself, *skip dessert for supper and you'll be back on track.*

"Are you Jane?" a voice called from the edge of the pool. I squinted, since I'd taken my contacts out for the swim. "My name's Brian, Brian Kise."

Brian Kise, state diving champ. All-American nine times. I knew who he was. He'd even been my diving coach when he was in college and I was in eighth grade. Back then, he'd seemed a bit arrogant, with all his championships on top of basic good looks. He never demonstrated dives like the other coach or even put on a swimsuit. He'd kept me on the beginner squad because I'd blown a back somersault during a tryout night. I'd liked our other coach better.

"Hi," I said, not very enthusiastically.

"I saw you on the boards and asked Bob who you were." Bob had been the college coach for years. "He said you're graduating next month?"

I managed to make small talk for a few minutes, all the while thinking of my eighth-grade experiences with him. The way he looked at me . . . I *knew* he was going to call the college switchboard, get my number, and ask me out. What would I say if he called? Would I be in for an entire evening of Mr. State Champion's best diving-meet memories? I'd almost quit the team over that back somersault . . . but he *was* pretty cute.

The unwritten rule of dating is that the guy has to phone by Wednesday if he wants to ask you out for Saturday. Much sooner and he's too eager. Any later and it seems like an afterthought. Brian called Thursday. Was he so sure any girl would say yes that he didn't plan ahead?

"I should have called last night," he began, "but I didn't get home from work early enough. By any chance are you free on Saturday? There's this neat little radio program over in St. Paul called *Prairie Home* . . ."

He'd heard of it? Hmmm, any evening with Garrison Keillor wouldn't be a total loss.

"And then we could go out for Chinese food . . ." My favorite . . .

"That sounds fun," I heard myself say. One date didn't mean we had to go out again. Besides, *Prairie Home* and Chinese . . .

The next morning as I walked into breakfast, one of my good friends looked at me and asked, "And why are you smirking?"

I explained, "My Saturday night plans are pretty good . . . a date for *Prairie Home*—"

"Did he suggest that or did you?"

"He did. And then a Chinese dinner—"

"Did he suggest that or did you?"

"He did."

"Who is this guy?" she said with a smirk probably very like the one I'd been wearing. After I explained, she shook her head and said, "You're going to marry him."

And I did.

I've never thought God made Brian offer *Prairie Home* and Chinese food as a way to say, *"Jane, this is the one. Marry him."* Instead, I think God was telling me, *"Forget your eighth-grade opinions. You've started slamming the door on relationships a bit too quickly. Give this guy a chance."*

———————

*Nearly twenty-five years later, we still listen to* A Prairie Home Companion *almost every Saturday night. As the theme song starts at 5 P.M., I smile, remembering how the show helped me look long and hard at a first date that was the chance of a lifetime.*

## A Neon Sign
### By Janelle Huston

Sometimes I think my first love was a thesaurus. As a little girl in pigtails, I was fascinated by my grandparents' library. Floor to ceiling, books lined the shelves, leather-bound sets interspersed with worn paperbacks and colorful cloth bindings. From *Aesop's Fables* to the *Zoology of Zaire* it was a world awaiting exploration. Clumsily clacking the keys of Grandfather's 1929 Underwood, I dreamed about becoming an author.

While other girls groaned over English assignments, I eagerly penned poetry and short stories. I agonized over college papers, yet knew I'd found my calling when a professor commented on an essay, "I hope you enjoyed writing this as much as I enjoyed reading it." Oh, I had!

But how to get published? Submit a story to an editor and wait and wait and wait until a slim envelope with a form rejection letter arrives in the mail? Even though my professors encouraged me to try, the image frightened me. So I only wrote for my own amusement. Scribblings on scraps of paper evolved into a children's story, *What Do You Do With A Blue Gnu?*

Having a friend's three-year-old exclaim, "Read it again!" was almost as good as seeing it in print.

My friend asked, "Why don't you publish that? It's as good as any of the books I've bought for him."

"You don't understand," I countered. "I don't decide to publish a book. I have to persuade an *editor* to publish my book."

"So?"

"And on my way I'll encounter a lot of editors who hate it. Why would I invite rejection into my life? I can get that at my current job."

Relentless, my friend said, "That's because you are in the wrong line of work. You should be a writer."

But I knew it wasn't that easy. No, if God really wanted me to be an author, I needed a clear sign. Otherwise, wouldn't my scribblings be a waste of time God would want me to use other ways?

For two years *The Blue Gnu* gathered dust on a shelf while I longed to make a career change. I prayed, *Lord, give me an answer.* Meanwhile, I took an extra job working with special-needs children. Exhausted one evening after a marathon session of reading Dr. Seuss to them, I flipped on PBS to clear the rhythm and rhyme from my head. Instead, a documentary on the yak-raising, yurt-dwelling nomads of Asia inspired another children's book, *Help! There's a Yak in My Yurt!*

Submit it, though? I confided to a friend how scared I was to slip that manuscript into an envelope. "Why doesn't God give unmistakable answers to prayer anymore?" I mourned.

Chuckling, my friend said, "If you saw a blazing azalea on the drive home, how would you interpret it? Dozens of people have told you to try publishing and you're still waiting for God to set foliage on fire. Submit your work and ask God to open wide the door of opportunity. Then add, 'If publication isn't part of your plan for me, close the door tight.' It's a scary prayer," he admitted. "You'll have to knock on some doors."

That night I prayed that prayer, finally grasping that God couldn't guide me if I wasn't moving. Over the next weeks, I researched how to submit manuscripts, called a former Sunday school teacher who was an author and retired magazine editor, and joined a group called the Minnesota Christian Writers Guild.

My first submission was actually an entry in the Guild's annual contest, a story about an enormous old English mastiff named Clifford. As I entered the next meeting, I prayed, *Okay, God, I'm moving now. Can I have that neon-sign answer? Did I win the contest?*

Our speaker began, "Some authors are so talented that when I read their stuff, I feel like chucking my computer and taking up yak ranching."

I choked on my coffee. Yak ranching! What are the chances that she would reference yak ranching? *Oh, come on, it's just a coincidence,* I told myself.

But as I left the meeting I stopped in the church lobby to look at what I thought was a large kiosk covered with posters. The first sign I read, though, informed me that it was a yurt the church would be donating to earthquake victims in a developing nation. A yurt in a Minnesota church? Yak ranching?

I turned to share these coincidences with a fellow writer, to get a second opinion, when the missions information board caught my eye. Right in the middle was a Brahma bull whose horns had been painted blue to match the ox cart he pulled in his native India. Awfully close to a blue gnu, don't you think?

Driving to work Monday morning, I prayed, *I think I'm hearing your answer, God, that maybe I can keep working on children's books. But what about my Clifford story? If it's not too much to ask . . .*

The thought was hardly complete when a Scholastic Books Truck swung around the corner. On its side was a picture of one of their best-selling book characters, Clifford, the Big Red Dog. Laughing out loud, I prayed, *Okay, God, I get it. It's all right if I write!*

It may be years before I publish anything significant, but those flashing neon yaks and yurts assured me that I'm not wasting my time—or God's time. I'll have fun writing, and my friends' children can laugh at *The Blue Gnu* while I enjoy the journey, no matter where it leads.

————

*Janelle Huston has many more anecdotes as amazing and amusing as this one. Employed as a Communications Associate writing procedure manuals and newsletter articles, she is currently seeking a publisher for her Gnu and Yak children's stories and two new ones,* Libby the Lobster and the Selfish Shellfish *and* Zachary's Patchwork Heart. *Janelle also writes humor and inspirational pieces for adults.*

## A Swirl of Purple
*By Pamela Haskin*

"Did you bring the list?" Mom asked as I slid into the backseat and shut the door.

"Right here!" I said, waving the yellow paper in the air that listed half a dozen dress shops that carried a line of bridal dresses.

On the way out of town we picked up Betty, whom I affectionately call my other mother. "Hi, darlin'," she said as she climbed in the front. She reached over the seat and patted my hand. "We are going to have such fun today!"

"Do you really have your heart set on bright purple dresses?" I asked Mom. "What about a deep maroon instead?"

"You and Betty have to wear purple! I can see everything in my head already. Me in my red wedding dress. You walking me down the aisle in purple." Then to Betty she said, "Didn't I tell you she would fuss about purple?" They laughed.

I caught Betty's eye in the mirror of her downturned visor, hoping to see an inkling of support for my side. "I love purple!" she said with a teasing grin.

*Purple! One more thing to make me uncomfortable . . . Lord, if you can come up with a dress that the three of us can agree on, I'll know this marriage was meant to be,* I prayed, only half jokingly.

Quite honestly, a bit of uneasiness lingered in my mind. From my viewpoint, Mom was rushing into this marriage. She and I had grown very close in the six years since Dad had died. I didn't think she would ever get married again. She and Dad had been married almost forty years when he died. Theirs had not been an easy marriage. Dad's addiction to alcohol during most of those years had made life difficult for the whole family, more so for Mom, I knew.

But in these last few years, laughter bubbled easily from her as if a great weight had been lifted. In fact, she and Betty were known around town as "the laughin' ladies." What fun I had on my yearly trip down to see Mom. One day not long after Dad died, Mom announced, "I've never really liked cooking, so I'm giving it up." After that, we ate out every day. We shopped. We stayed up late talking and giggling like schoolgirls.

I came to know a whole different side of my mother. At least once each trip, she and Betty and I spent the whole day at Thelma's Place getting manicures and pedicures. Mom even talked Thelma into making our lunch in her tiny kitchen in the back room. We laughed the whole time we were there. Who knew Mom could be this much fun! She wasn't like that when I lived with her.

Then everything suddenly changed. Wendell! You can imagine my surprise when Mom canceled dinner plans with me one night. "Don't get the wrong idea! This is not a date," Mom assured me. "It's just Wendell. We're just friends going to get something to eat."

"Sounds like a date to me," I teased.

Wendell, recently widowed himself, really was a friend. For thirty years he and his family had lived in our same small town. I had gone to school with his kids. He had been a loving husband to his wife, and he served as a deacon in his church. None of this quelled my doubts, however, as I saw him and Mom growing closer.

Mom and Wendell went out almost every day over the next six weeks or so. As they spent more and more time together it quickly became obvious that they were now more than just friends.

Alarm bells clanged in my head one day when I found Mom working in the kitchen. "You're cooking?"

"Wendell really likes sweet-potato pancakes, so I'm making some for him," Mom said with a lilt in her voice. I raised my eyebrows. "It was my idea!" she added. "Wendell told me if I don't want to cook I don't have to. He'll take me out to eat every day if necessary!"

I couldn't quibble with how Wendell treated Mom, but I had other, very real concerns. Wendell was seventy-one years old, eight years older than Mom—she could so easily be widowed again. And he had had open-heart surgery some years before, even if he did play golf almost every afternoon. Further, they started making wedding plans after only a couple of months of dating—too fast to be rational, I thought. *Lord, I want only the best for my mother. She does seem happy. She wants me to walk her down the aisle, as you know. It would mean so much more if I could fully support her choice. How can I know that you have your hand in this marriage? Please, Lord, make me able to support her in her decision.*

"How about dark forest green dresses?" I threw out. It'd be so much easier to look happy during the wedding if I could at least wear something more subdued.

"Purple!" both my mothers shot back at me.

Mom, Betty, and I pushed through the doors of the first store on our list. Just inside the door stood a rack of dresses on clearance. I stared, not believing my eyes. Hanging on the backside were three purple dress suits. "Just what I had in mind!" Mom sang out. She pulled one of them off the rack and thrust it at me.

I held it to my neck, catching a glimpse of myself in the store window. A dark, regal shade of purple; clean, simple lines and no frills; just one visible button at the neck that somehow fit my conservative style. *I guess I can wear purple! This shade of purple, anyway.* "I love it!" I said honestly. "And it's my size," I added as I checked the tag.

The second dress had a missing button, so I handed the third one to Betty. *This just can't be,* my practical mind practically shouted at me.

"It's perfect! And it's my size!" Betty said.

*What were the chances of that? Thank you, Lord! I get your message loud and clear.* As Betty and I twirled in a swirl of purple in front of a three-way mirror, I caught Mom's eye. She smiled as unchecked tears wetted her cheeks. In that instant I knew that God had given me a sign, helping my heart and mind accept what I'd been seeing—that Mom and Wendell were right for each other. Goose bumps rose on my arms and suddenly a calm assurance took the place of doubt. Now I could walk my mother down the aisle in wholehearted support of a union that was meant to be!

———————

*"I could not have picked a better man myself for my mother," Pam says of Wendell. "They are so happy together." Pam continues her yearly trip to Texas to see her mother, and now Wendell. The rest of the time she is at home in the Alaskan bush, where she and her husband are participants in the Homestead Program administered by the State of Alaska. "Choose your own dream and go live it," she encourages those who come to listen to her speak. You can read all about her unusual and oftentimes humorous life in* A Deliberate Life: A Journey into the Alaskan Wilderness.

## KEY: God guides each one of us gently in ways we can best understand.

Radio shows, yurts, and bridesmaids' dresses can all be signs, but how do you know what to pay attention to and what to ignore? It's easy to fall into one of two traps:

- People who are certain that God *never* guides us directly ignore this truth: The Holy Spirit is already within us to guide us. Perhaps because they've seen the sensational side of this guidance system so misused, they choose to ignore concrete experiences others have had where the Spirit got their attention. These kinds of signs are best understood when we consider them as the whisper of the Holy Spirit who already resides within us.

- People who think God *always* gives us signs often ignore the other guidance systems. Because they are looking for *direct* leadings, they may miss what God has already told them in the Bible about the situation—or what God is saying through how they are gifted or through the counsel of others.

None of the writers of these stories received signs that told their future. Instead, they received general commands. *Keep writing. Take another look. Trust your mother.* They had to keep moving to see where those actions would lead. They could move ahead, though, confident that their actions were within God's moral bounds.

*Lord, you are everywhere*
  *in everything*
  *surrounding us, within us, ahead of us.*
*Your instruments of guidance are infinite.*
*Open my eyes to your leadings,*
  *let me hear your wisdom for me.*
*Yet guard me from confusion*
  *and from waiting for a sign*
  *when you've already shown me the way. Amen.*

---

[1]Matthew 13:16

# 7

# Doesn't God Open Doors?

**Key: Open doors don't necessarily point to God's will. Closed doors don't necessarily mean a certain path isn't God's will.**

*David, once a simple shepherd boy, knew he'd be king of Israel. How could he forget the day the great prophet Samuel had anointed him?*

*But there was one problem. Israel already had a king—King Saul—also anointed by Samuel. Even though Saul had disobeyed God and lost God's blessing, for now he still had the crown.*

*Saul was glad enough when David helped defeat the Philistines, but then the people celebrated by singing, "Saul has slain his thousands; and David his tens of thousands." That was the start of Saul's plotting against David's life. An all-out pursuit began—and continued for TEN YEARS. David fled Saul from town to town and into the deserts, an outlaw in the country where he would be king. Others joined him until he had an army of around four hundred men. So what did David do when Saul stumbled into the very cave where he was hiding?*

---

David leaned back against the cave wall, a cool relief from the noonday sun. His men sprawled about him in the darkness at the back of the cave. He was tired. Tired of running through the hills and the craggy rocks that he knew as only a shepherd could. Where was Saul now, and his army, three thousand strong?

Footsteps echoed from the front of the cave. David started. Of course, if he knew of this place, others would too. They were trapped. But one of his men, closer to the front, motioned to David to come forward.

Slowly, quietly, David crept along the cave wall until he could see the grotto at the mouth of the cave. There, a tall man was spreading his cloak out over a smooth area in the floor. The armor, his height . . . David caught sight of his face. It was Saul, also seeking relief from the heat of the day.

At first, no one dared move or say a word, but soon the king's breathing told David's men that Saul was asleep. One of David's men whispered, "This is it! The Lord has placed your enemy in your hand to deal with as you wish!"

*It must be true,* thought David. He thought of all the attempts Saul had made on his life. Surely his years of exile were finally coming to an end. He unsheathed his knife and crept silently toward Saul.

The king slept on. David knelt beside him, raised the knife, and paused, staring at the blade that he'd used so many times as a leader of Saul's armies. He thought of the evenings he'd played the harp for Saul, soothing the troubled king's soul. The same hands that had anointed David as king had anointed the man who lay helpless before him. Quickly, he cut off a corner of Saul's robe and returned to where his men waited.

His men stared at him in disbelief. "Why didn't you kill him? This may be your only chance!"

David hushed them and whispered, "How could I lift my hand against the Lord's anointed? Who was I even to take this corner from his tunic? But later, I'll show it to him so he will recognize that he has nothing to fear from me. Then maybe our exile will be over."

With that, David again leaned back against the wall of the cave, his heart lifted in prayer as he waited for Saul to leave their refuge. How he wished he could play his harp as words of praise formed in his mind:

I cry out to God Most High,
to God, who fulfills his purpose for me.
He sends from heaven and saves me,
rebuking those who hotly pursue me;
God sends his love and his faithfulness. . . .
For great is your love, reaching to the heavens;
your faithfulness reaches to the skies.[1]

―――――

*The heading to Psalm 57 tells us that David composed it when he had fled from Saul into the cave. He must have hesitated when he saw Saul, sleeping, vulnerable right in front of him. An open door to the kingship he'd already been promised? Who wouldn't contemplate that possibility?*

*Yet David knew that a bloody start to his reign could compromise everything that followed. In the Bible, open doors don't always mean "Walk through with God's blessing." David knew that, so he waited.*

*Further, closed doors don't always mean "Don't go there. Stop!" Patriarchs, prophets, and apostles keep moving despite obstacle after obstacle. The same is true today. You have to read much deeper than the mere facts of a situation. You are trying to read what God is telling you in the situation. For David, perhaps God was saying, I, not Saul, am in charge here, even though you've been on the run so long.*

*In the next stories, you'll see doors that are wide open, ajar, stuck fast, and others where people can't seem to agree which way they're hinged. As you read, consider that until you hold lightly to your own hopes and plans, you can't hear whether God is opening or closing the door for you.*

Your love is ever before me, and I walk continually in your truth.[2]


## Who's in Charge?
*By Jeff Dyson*

Our home seemed surreal, shadowy, silent, as I stood in the living room just after our three-year-old son's funeral. His favorite book still lay on the coffee table. I spotted a little car half tucked under the couch he'd used as a garage. Blake had died suddenly of meningitis. I caught my breath, trying not to start crying again. Why hadn't I taken his sudden fever more seriously? What if I'd rushed him to the hospital even an hour sooner? I had failed my family and my beloved son in the worst possible way.

My wife, Pat, wrapped her arms around me and whispered, "We'll have another baby." I stiffened slightly, then returned her hug. Pat wasn't trying to replace Blake. She already knew that we needed to fill our home again with the sounds of running feet and childish laughter, for our sake and the sake of our two older sons.

Pat was ready before I was; I felt that our fragile emotions needed healing before our lives again revolved around a newborn. Conceiving Blake and his two older brothers had been easy, so I assumed that we'd have a short nine-month wait.

Instead, months passed without Pat's becoming pregnant. Finally we saw a fertility specialist. He put Pat on a merry-go-round of pills, shots, and ultrasounds.

A year after Blake's death we rejoiced that Pat was pregnant, only to grieve again when she miscarried early on. The doctor gently told us our chances of conceiving again were slim.

A deep sadness settled over our home. Our sons tiptoed around like they were in a museum. Occasionally, I found them playing with Blake's games and puzzles. Their grief was as sharp as ours.

Things were just as grim at the family hardware store I owned. Sales dipped considerably after an oil bust. Making matters worse, a road-widening project closed the street in front of the store for three months. Even some of our most faithful customers told me, "We'll be back, but for now it's too much of a hassle."

Putting bread on my own table became a real concern—and I had fifty employees depending on me. I couldn't think straight, couldn't seem to make decisions. *Help me with these challenges, Lord,* I prayed as I reviewed our falling receipt figures. *I'm not measuring up.* Secretly, I wondered if I could have handled the extra pressure of another child if Pat *hadn't* miscarried. Maybe this was all God's timing.

I dragged in from work one day, my mind consumed with business woes. Pat engulfed me in a huge hug before I even kicked off my shoes. "Guess what, Jeff," she beamed. "My friend Cathy and her husband are opening an adoption agency. We're on her list of prospective parents. Isn't that great?"

"Adoption?" I said. *Adoption?*

Pat's face radiated hope. Slowly I answered, "I'd never really thought about it, but I guess that would be okay."

With a loving poke at my chest, Pat quipped, "We just want a child, right? It doesn't matter how the baby gets here!"

She was right. Each morning we ended our prayer with ". . . and please, God, grant us a child." I guess I still hoped we'd be able to conceive after all.

"Adoption could be good, babe," I said. "What's the wait, a couple of years?" Surely business would be back on track before anything came of this.

"Maybe as little as a year," Pat said. "Oh, Jeff, I just know adoption is what God has in mind for us. I feel so at peace about it!"

I hugged my wife, my mind already drifting back to business problems.

Five short months passed. Pat called me at work in the middle of the day. "Jeff!" she shrieked. "We've got a little girl! I've seen her and she's beautiful and she's ours!"

"What? Whoa, gal," I said. My stomach flipped. Weren't we still months away from this? "I'll come home for lunch and we can talk."

Pat set plates filled with lovely salad and fresh rolls in front of each of us, but she didn't touch hers. She talked nonstop. "Her parents are just teenagers, never used drugs or alcohol. They tried to keep her a secret, so she was born at home. Oh, Jeff—she's got dark, curly hair, cries like a little kitten, she's so tiny. But she was full term. Honey, she's the most beautiful baby you've ever seen. Well, right now she's hooked up to tubes and monitor because of severe jaundice—"

"Jaundice?" A warning bell rang in my mind. "Isn't that serious?"

"Sometimes there can be permanent liver or brain damage, and there aren't any guarantees . . . but her doctor says she's alert and lively and I just know she's going to be okay!"

"Pat," I said, "that's a red flag if ever I've seen one. A sick baby after all we've been through? What if she doesn't make it? And how about our finances? Another college fund? You know how bad business has been. Besides, I think it's too soon. We're all still grieving over Blake."

My wife looked at me in disbelief as the objections flowed from me. "I can't believe what I'm hearing, Jeff. Don't you see? This little girl is an answer to our prayers! God opened a door for us—now, don't tell me you're not willing to walk through it!"

"An open door? With the risks involved? I'm not sure you're seeing clearly right now."

"Maybe your vision should include *God's* vision for our family!" Pat retorted. "Now, I'm going back to visit our little girl. Will you come with me?"

I looked down at my plate. "Can't, babe. I've got a two-o'clock meeting. I'll be home about seven."

Pat didn't answer, nor did she kiss me good-bye. She was furious, but I was just plain scared. Pat wasn't being rational, so I needed to examine every angle. A sick baby? I just couldn't see it.

Over the next week Pat visited the baby at the hospital daily, gushing more each night, "The way her eyelashes curl up and—oh, I swear she smiled at me today!"

I made excuses not to go with her and wondered whether Pat should be going so much. I'd asked a doctor friend of mine about severe jaundice. He answered frankly, "I don't like the sound of that, Jeff. There could be lifelong problems. I wouldn't chance it." I knew he was right.

That night, I recounted our conversation to Pat and learned that she'd asked the hospital neonatologist to do some tests. The results confirmed that chances of permanent damage from the jaundice were small.

Then she added, "The nurses told me she isn't gaining weight fast enough; they're worried she has failure-to-thrive syndrome. She needs a *home*. How she'd thrive here!"

Pat cried and begged me to at least go and see the baby. I stared at the floor, my heart pounding. "Pat, I just can't."

The next morning, Pat prayed, "God, give us a push in the direction you want us to go with this baby." I wasn't fooled. When she said *us*, I knew she meant *Jeff*.

During the day, my mind kept drifting to the tiny girl in the hospital. My wife's words rang in my ears all day. *Dark, curly hair and chubby chipmunk cheeks . . . She needs us as much as we need her . . . God will provide for her financially . . .* Pesky woman! I couldn't get her eyes, filled with love for that baby, out of my thoughts!

All day between cutting pipe and selling weed eaters, I agonized. Finally I went to my desk, sat down, and bowed my head. "God," I said, "I'm so afraid I'm going to foul up. So I'm putting you in charge. Please show me your will for my family and for this little girl."

That night, Pat didn't even mention the baby. We joined our extended family at a local restaurant. As laughter circled the table, I felt more relaxed than I had in months.

At the table next to ours, an adorable little girl, about six months old, sat in a high chair, smiling as she slid bits of cracker around and tapped her spoon on the tray. I couldn't keep my eyes off her. Pat saw me watching her but said nothing.

As we left the restaurant, several people exclaimed, "Look at that!" "Have you ever seen one so brilliant?" "Or so big?"

A gigantic rainbow stretched from one side of the sky to the other.

Pat's eyes met mine and I could read her mind. *A sign!* A sign of God's promises.

Suddenly a voice said, "Let's go see her." *My* voice! How light and carefree I felt!

As we drove to the hospital, Pat asked, "What changed your mind?"

"You wore me down," I said.

"No, sweetheart," my wife beamed. "*God* wore you down."

At the hospital Pat handed me the fragile slip of a girl she was determined would be ours. Tiny as she was, the baby grabbed my finger and squeezed with the grip of a prizefighter. That squeeze won me over. How could she ever be anything but Daddy's girl?

The next day Pat dressed her in a frilly pink dress befitting the princess she was, and we took her home to an adoring family. She has healed our hearts and brought us indescribable joy. Fifteen years later, I continue to thank God for being in charge, for wearing me down, for giving us a beautiful, intelligent, healthy daughter—our Melissa.

———

*After adopting Melissa, Jeff and Pat asked to adopt another child, but the agency said no. "You've got three children, some people have none. Don't be greedy," they were told.*

*Four and a half years later, a young couple stopped by the agency, looked through the pictures of prospective families, and picked out Jeff and Pat. Adamantly, Pat accompanied the expectant mother to all of her doctor's appointments. She and Jeff named their newest addition Brooke. "God meant for her to be ours," says Jeff. "The second time around, I had no trouble recognizing that it was a God thing!"*

*Brooke, now ten, enjoys dancing, playing the piano with big sis, Melissa, and being an aunt to Jeff and Pat's young grandsons, Wes and Ty. "Life is great when you put God in charge," affirms Jeff.*

## My Heart Said *Go*
*By Dodie Davis*

As I walked briskly up the stairs to my second-floor apartment I noted, *You're getting used to this place; it's almost like home.* Months before, when my marriage of twenty-seven years crumbled, I didn't think I'd ever feel at home again. I'd stayed in our little town to be near my supportive circle of friends. One of my four daughters lived close by as well. Tough as things had been, my life had some normalcy again. I'd even started teaching fifth grade at our church's Christian school.

My phone was ringing; I dashed up the last few stairs. "Hello!" I answered.

"Mom, it's Kristy." My third daughter and her husband, John, lived a few hundred miles away in Minnesota.

"I'm so frightened," she continued, choking off a sob. "I had an MRI today—there's a brain tumor. The doctor thinks it's benign, but he'll biopsy it after the baby is born. Mom, I'm only twenty-four. . . ."

The view out my window blurred. Kristy had two little girls and was expecting a third child. *Why was the sun still shining? How could a bird sing, or a child laugh? Shouldn't everything stop? Please, Lord, not my daughter.*

The next months passed in hope and anxiety. Kristy's pregnancy brought a healthy baby girl. When I visited her hospital room two little voices piped up. "Grandma, come see our new baby." Kristy sat up in bed holding the baby while three-year-old Heather and two-year-old Mary Rose snuggled next to her. Proud grins spread across their faces. I prayed that nothing would change that picture of happiness.

The first biopsy reports *were* hopeful. Kristy told me, "The tumor's benign! They can't operate, though, because of its location. So they'll just keep watching it."

Throughout the next year, medication controlled Kristy's slight seizures, and she thrived caring for her three little girls. Then my phone rang again. This time it was John.

"Kristy had a bad seizure that lasted most of the night. She's in the hospital."

Another biopsy revealed a dreadfully aggressive tumor. John's voice shook as he described the chemotherapy and radiation regimen they hoped would slow its progress.

"Oh, John," I managed to whisper, fighting the sobs rising in my throat. I couldn't think, couldn't speak.

"Mom, are you there?" John's concerned voice refocused my thoughts. My hand was gripping the phone so tightly that it hurt. I forced myself to take a deep breath. "I'm here. How can I help?"

Hesitantly, he answered, "Kristy—and I—want you here, for Kristy's sake as much as to help with the girls. But you just settled in to your job and apartment. It's asking too much."

I knew what my heart wanted—to be with Kristy. But how? Break my teaching contract? Ask for a leave of absence? Would I ever come back? Where would I live—with them or in an apartment? Where would I work?

"John, my mind is swirling. I need to pray about this," I said. "I want to be near all of you, especially Kristy, but I need to make the right decision."

I thought of little else for days. One afternoon, my students worked quietly at their desks while I corrected math papers. My mind drifted. John's job involved travel. How would Kristy manage when the treatments sapped her strength? People from their church would help, but that's not the same as having your mother with you. Yet I couldn't desert my students. And how would I find employment in Minnesota? *God, how will I know where you want me to be?*

The sounds of whispering and coughs brought me back to my classroom. I looked up. At least ten hands waved impatiently in the air, pointing at the clock. "What is it?" I asked.

"We're supposed to be in gym class, Mrs. Davis."

That night as I prayed, I remembered a familiar verse, "If any of you lacks wisdom, he should ask God."[3] *Lord,* I thought, *I really do need your wisdom.*

The following Saturday morning I sat down at my kitchen table with a steaming cup of coffee and a legal pad. I drew a line down the middle of the paper. Under "Reasons to Stay" I wrote: (1) Good job that meets financial needs, (2) Doing what I love—teaching children, (3) Pleasant, affordable apartment, (4) Another daughter, Dawn, and husband close by, (5) Friends, (6) If I move, I will have to find a job and a place to live.

Under "Reasons to Move" I wrote, *Kristy needs me.*

Common sense told me that because I had no financial cushion, I couldn't move without a job. Yet, how could I work and still help Kristy? John might be out of town during a serious seizure. Besides, how could I transport her to doctor appointments *and* hold a job? *God, this is so complicated.*

The date for renewing my teaching contract loomed closer. I had to decide. Then one night the phone rang.

"Hi, Dodie, this is Pastor Bob." Kristy's pastor. Was something wrong?

Much to my relief he continued, "John mentioned your quandary over moving here and—maybe this will help. Our part-time church secretary is leaving, and we want to hire a full-time replacement. The pay won't be great, but it might be sufficient."

I asked a few questions about the job. He filled me in and added, "We know what John and Kristy are facing; you'll be free to leave the office whenever they need you."

When I hung up the phone, I looked around my apartment. *Say good-bye, you'll soon be in Minnesota,* I realized. Surely God was opening a door by solving my biggest problem. *Thank you, Father,* I prayed, *for pointing the way.*

The last weeks of school flew by. My daughter Dawn came over early one Saturday morning to help pack. She laughed at the stacks of boxes everywhere. "Wow, Mom, we've got work to do!"

We wrapped and packed for several hours and then took a break. I had just poured us each a cup of coffee when the phone rang.

"Dodie, this is Pastor Bob again. I'm so sorry . . ." he began, his voice filled with concern. Because of financial troubles, the secretarial position would be part time, no benefits. "I know Kristy and John were depending on you . . . I hope things work out."

I hung up the phone, confused. *God—shouldn't I be with Kristy? I was so sure that you'd provided that church job. Did I miss your plan? Am I supposed to stay here?*

The following evening after supper I sat down at the kitchen table with my Bible, pen, and paper, and looked up every verse I could find on God's will. The summer sun's rays faded into darkness as I read and reread certain verses:

> . . . *for it is God who works in you to will and to act according to his good purpose.*[4]
>
> *Do not be conformed to this world, but be transformed by the renewing of your minds, so that you may discern what is the will of God.*[5]

God's will worked from within me, helping me discern what to do? Then . . . my desire to be with Kristy could be God's purposes working within me? *I think I understand, Lord. Maybe this isn't a closed door, but my opportunity to instead ignore what the world tells me about needing a job, trust you, and push through in spite of the obstacles.*

I moved to Minnesota. That summer with Kristy and John affirmed my decision. Chemotherapy and radiation left Kristy weak, sick, and tired. Each evening I readied tiny Alicia for bed and laid her in Kristy's arms for her "night-night" bottle. While they snuggled, John and I helped the two older girls don pajamas, brush teeth, and settle in for a bedtime story. Then I sat on the couch and rubbed Kristy's burned and itching bare scalp. "Mom, I don't know what we'd do without you," she murmured almost nightly.

The part-time church job turned into full time at the end of the summer, answering my prayers for security. I'd only needed faith to trust that my desire to be with Kristy was God-given, even if the path to get there wasn't clear. Moving forward by faith allowed me to spend the last eight years of Kristy's life with her. I have never stopped being thankful for the assurance God's Word gave me, even in confusing circumstances.

---

*Dodie soon acquired a wonderful group of supportive friends in Minnesota. She is presently writing a book that includes Kristy's story. God has given her opportunities to teach Bible classes, speak at women's conferences, and give Bible storytelling workshops all over the country. She lives near John and her granddaughters and is able to be part of their lives.*

## Finding My Way Home
### *By Deb Richards*

"In essence, for the past three months you've allowed your wife to live out of her car, dependent on the kindness of friends and strangers." The voice belonged to my attorney.

"Yes," my husband answered.

I held my breath, not daring to look at the judge, praying that he'd recognize my needs.

"And your life remained virtually the same during those three months?"

"Yes," he answered once more.

Homeless. That's what I'd become. But for too long I'd resisted the idea of leaving my husband, attempting to reconcile the fact of my mate's infidelity with the truth that God hates divorce.

I'd prayed for God to intervene, for my husband to turn around. Finally, overwhelmed by his emotional brutality, I escaped for a weekend, seeking refuge at my friend Kay's.

During one of our conversations, Kay said, "Deb, whenever I've prayed for you lately, I picture you at a convent or retreat center."

I smiled but shook my head. Of course my "retreat buddy" would suggest this. Over the years, we'd explored many such places together.

Kay pressed further. "That Trappestine place near Dubuque has a work program, remember?"

Move to Dubuque, so far from home? *What home?* I reminded myself.

Our home, particularly the sanctuary of my backyard, had been sacred ground to me, providing the private space I needed to paint and write, grow flowers, and hear God. Yet I had to admit that staying hadn't helped my marriage.

Kay's concern, along with the fact that she knew me so well, gave weight to her suggestion. I began praying about the possibility as I drove away. During the next days, I pondered going someplace emotionally safe while I waited for my husband's change of heart. And I spoke with my husband. If he didn't end his relationship with the other woman, I would make arrangements to leave. He didn't believe me.

Finally I called a priest and shared Kay's idea. Did he know where I might go? He recommended the Trappestine Abbey in Dubuque—the same one Kay had mentioned—but gave me a list of some others.

When I called, the abbey's work program was completely booked! I lay on the bed and wept, my fragile confidence shattered. Then I heard a gentle whisper in my ear. *"Maybe that's not where I want you to go."*

I sat up. Next on the list was Shalom, a retreat center.

"We don't have a work program," the director explained. We both waited, pensive. Then, "Why don't you come ahead? We'll find something for you to do."

Three days later I placed Shalom's phone number on my husband's desk and packed my car with what I considered to be essentials—clothing and toiletries, books, my pillow, the angel candle from my girlfriends, some photographs. I added my Bible, journals, favorite pens, and watercolors.

Almost as an afterthought, I carefully placed a few potted flowering plants in the trunk. All pieces of home.

On my arrival Sister Marie-Therese showed me to my tiny room. Immediately, she recognized what I didn't: I was physically, emotionally, and spiritually depleted. "Rest, not work, is what you need," she said firmly. "And food for body and soul."

Slowly, in that place of refuge, God helped me relinquish my home and my marriage. I remember praying, *God, I see why you led me here, but what is next? I have nowhere to go when they need my room for others in a few weeks.*

When a friend called a few days later and asked me to house-sit while she was on vacation, I laughed at God's timing.

Then a retired couple asked me to care for their furnished house through the winter months. Their lovely home offered a view of the river and safe paths for long walks.

In that solitary place I took time to grieve my losses. Over and over, the promises of Jeremiah ran through my mind: *"For I know the thoughts and plans that I have for you, says the Lord, thoughts and plans for welfare and peace and not for evil, to give you hope in your final outcome."* [6]

But hope in what? My old life had been stolen from me. I had no idea how to replace it. How could God fill my empty future with new thoughts and plans if my present moments were so hollow and meaningless?

Slowly, as my grief eased, I concentrated my prayer time more on listening for what might come next. God helped me reach out for the new people, new experiences, and new possibilities.

In November I attended a writer's conference. One evening, when we gathered to pray, I asked for clear direction from God—especially about where I would live once my divorce was final.

Women in the group prayed, "Lord, make your will so clear that Deb won't question it. Bring it right to her doorstep!"

Eventually spring arrived, along with my divorce decree. The house where I'd been living would be sold. In late April my friend Jane and I walked the bike path along the Mississippi. "After a year of being displaced," I shared, "I'm sure I'm ready for my own home."

Impulsively, I looked up into the sky and said, "Lord, could you please bring me a house by May first? Now, really, how hard would that be for you?"

Jane stopped in her tracks, laughing. "Do you really talk to God like that?" she blurted.

I stopped too. It felt good to laugh. "God gave me this sense of humor," I assured Jane, not joking in the least. Secretly I wondered, *Is it time? Do I really trust that God will do this for me?*

A few moments later, a young man on in-line blades handed us a flyer: HOUSE FOR SALE. I stared at the picture. Could this be my answer? Jane and I jumped in the car and drove over to see.

The huge house stood on an exposed corner lot with traffic whizzing by on both sides. Definitely not a house for Deb, we decided! Still, a sliver of light slipped through a door in my thinking. *God is taking my desire seriously.*

On Sunday morning, the last day of April, I returned from church to find a newspaper lying on the front porch. I didn't subscribe to the paper!

Eagerly, I sat on the steps and opened the real estate section. I'd already decided on the neighborhood and price range for "my" house. But there was nothing there. Nothing. *I'm wrong,* I thought as I folded the paper and walked indoors.

Later that afternoon, I mulled things over and prayed. *Surely it's time, God. What about the flyer the other day? I thought you were trying to tell me something. And what about this newspaper?*

I looked through the ads again. This time I noticed a "For Sale By Owner" ad, with an open house from 1 to 4. "My" neighborhood and "my" price range! I didn't dare believe it. I glanced at the clock. It was four-thirty.

I phoned the number in the ad and spoke with Cathy, the house's owner. I could come at six-thirty, when she got home from church. I drove over to see the outside! (Okay, I'll admit I peeked in the window, too.) The charming Cape Cod was newly painted with a small, low-maintenance yard and a screened-in porch. I imagined myself writing there, and painting.

Two hours later, as I walked from room to room, the full suitability of this simple house astounded me. There were enough built-in bookcases to hold my library of books. My small collection of furniture would fit exactly, right down to the new writing desk I'd found. I gazed out the window at a beautifully landscaped private yard, backing up to a wildlife-abundant ravine!

I knew I'd make an offer, although we agreed not to finalize anything for a few days. Possibly someone else would offer Cathy more money. Then I raced home and called Jane. "I found my house!" I practically shouted into the phone.

The following morning, Cathy called. "I took the sign out of the yard. I just have a feeling," she explained. "I want you to have the house."

Later that week, when I went over to measure some rooms, Cathy confided, "After we signed the papers, I had a barrage of calls, mostly from people who were out of town over the weekend. One woman even offered to give me cash if I would sell it to her! Of course, I refused."

With gratitude, I realized that God had reserved this place just for me, and brought me to it! As I walked to the car, I recalled my earlier fears—of leaving home and never finding a place that was right for me. I remembered the newspaper I'd found on my front porch—the newspaper I didn't even subscribe to. And I recalled the prayer of a stranger, "Lord, make your will so clear to Deb that she won't question it. Bring it right to her doorstep!"

––––––––––

*Eighteen months after moving into her "peaceful dwelling place," Deb was making plans to remarry. One afternoon she stopped in the driveway to admire her next-door neighbor's new baby. Kari was surprised to learn that Deb was moving but told Deb that friends of hers wanted to move into the neighborhood. A few days later, Kari's friends stopped by and purchased Deb's house! Deb is happily remarried and lives in Minnesota with her husband, Jack Richards. She loves her new backyard!*

## KEY: Open doors don't necessarily point to God's will. Closed doors don't necessarily mean a certain path isn't God's will.

As you ponder what God might be telling you through the events of your life, instead of asking whether a door is open or closed, ask, "God, what are you trying to tell me?"

Perhaps God wants you to give up the burden of being in charge, like Jeff.

Perhaps God wants you to trust your own values and step forward, like Dodie, before all the pieces fall into place.

Perhaps God wants you to change a belief, as Deb did concerning her true home.

Or perhaps, like King David, you need to see that God is still with you, even if your circumstances make you wonder if you somehow missed God's plan.

All of this means we need to hold lightly to our own plans. The word *Lord* has no meaning unless you sometimes go directions you wouldn't choose on your own. God might just as easily require a hard task as an easy one.

So when you see a door, open or closed, ask, "God, this is what I see. This is what I'm feeling about it and what I think the Bible tells me. Am I getting it right?" Ask people whose wisdom you trust how they might evaluate your circumstances. Check what you are seeing against your own gifts and special design. Worry less if you know your actions will further God's work.

In short, let circumstances light your path rather than shadow your vantage point, yet know that you can walk on, relying on other ways that God guides you when it seems too dark to see.

*Was that you, Lord, or did the wind slam that door?*
*I'm like David's men, seeing what I want to see,.*
> *hearing what I want to hear,*
> *forgetting that your way might be easy*
> *or hard.*
*Perhaps by closing my eyes I might still my soul*
> *long enough to hear you,*
> *long enough to learn whether to forge ahead*
> *or return by another way. Amen.*

---

[1]Psalm 57: 2–3, 10
[2]Psalm 26:3, a psalm of David
[3]James 1:5
[4]Philippians 2:13
[5]Romans 12:2 NRSV
[6]Jeremiah 29:11 AMP

# 8

# What If I Don't Think I Can Do What God Is Asking?

Key: The path before you may require the gifts of those around you.

*Moses was certainly one of the greatest leaders of Israel; in fact, the writer of Hebrews holds only Jesus as greater. But he couldn't do everything. He tried to use his lack of eloquence to escape telling Pharaoh to release the Israelites from slavery. God made it clear, though, that Moses had been given that task; he would take his brother Aaron along to speak the thoughts God would give him. Moses' gifts didn't limit the scope of the task God set before him; he just wasn't expected to do it alone. Moses learned what was possible when he obeyed God, even if the task seemed beyond his ability.*

*After the Exodus, Moses became the undisputed leader of Israel. Perhaps he'd learned his lesson well about leadership—it would be hard, dangerous, and exhausting. His new duties included acting as the interpreter of God's decrees and laws. Exodus 18:13–27 describes how Moses "took his seat to serve as judge for the people, and they stood around him from morning till evening."* [1]

---

Evening. Finally. The desert sun, already halfway behind the distant bluffs, cast its last warming rays across the rocky alcove where Moses had sat all day long. He'd listened to men and women recount their woes, ask about the Law, press him for guidance. But the line was just as long at the end of the day as at the start.

The whole endless process would start again as soon as the sun poked its face into the eastern sky. *Until then,* he thought, *I am not going to think, not going to talk, not—please Lord—going to be called into a dispute. Just the cool darkness of our own tent.*

But even as he pushed aside the cloths that shielded the entry, a voice spoke, "Moses? Is that you? I have a question." It was his father-in-law, Jethro, who was visiting.

Eyes bleary with fatigue, Moses stared at his father-in-law for a moment, then joined him, sinking down onto the rugs that formed the floor of the tent. *Not another question,* he protested to himself.

"Yes?" he answered, trying to hide his annoyance.

"I watched you for a while today," Jethro said. "Tell me, how many people spoke with you?"

Moses shrugged. "I didn't keep track."

"How many are still waiting?"

Faces skipped across Moses' memory. Arguments over a broken water jug. Complaints over whether tents were proper distances from the fires. Accusations of grave insults. "More than I care to think about," he answered.

Jethro leaned forward and caught his son-in-law's hand. "Then why are you sitting alone as judge?"

"Because . . . I'm—I'm the only one God has spoken to," Moses stammered. "The people depend on me."

Jethro snorted ever so slightly. "And how many questions today required simple common sense, not the word of God? Listen, you don't belong being the sole judge of Israel. You'll wear yourself out. You're too exhausted by noontime to be wise. And think of those who wait, some for days. How else could they have used their time? How can this be right?"

"Being God's leader has never made me popular," Moses sputtered. Then he held his breath for a moment, sensing that Jethro's motive was concern, not criticism. "Today, for example, two men were arguing again about God's directions concerning food. They vowed to only listen to me. Yes, it's hard on me, but since when has obeying God been easy?"

"But you could just hear the big disputes. Moses, you can't do everything. Yes, continue as teacher of God's law, judge over serious matters. As for the rest, every tribe already has men who are capable of leadership. Seek them out, those who ask God for wisdom, who won't take bribes.

Set the wisest over groups of a thousand people and have leaders of hundreds, fifties, and tens report to them."

Fatigue clouded Moses' thoughts. "They might make mistakes. . . ."

"As if you might not, exhausted as you are?" Jethro shook his head. "Ask God if my advice is sound. You *will* break down at this pace. And that won't help anyone."

Moses closed his eyes for a moment. *Just handle the important cases . . .*

"Make time for what you do best," Jethro murmured softly. "Teach people about the God you know. Teach them to depend on Yahweh, not just on you."

———

*Moses fell into the trap of thinking that just because God had asked him to do something, he had to do it alone. And everyone suffered: Moses as he wore himself out, those whose lives were on hold until they spoke with him, and those who couldn't develop their gifts of leadership as long as Moses was doing it all.*

*Sometimes following God means relying on those around us. Maybe you, like Moses, are on the verge of exhaustion, not asking whether others should be helping you. Or maybe you've been saying no to some task God wants you to take on, claiming, "God, there's no way I have the talent to carry that out." Remember, Moses made that mistake, too, claiming he couldn't speak to Pharaoh.*

*In the following stories, you'll walk alongside those who learned that sometimes what God is asking is too big for you alone. But it might not be too big to accomplish with the help of others.*

Two are better than one, because they have a good return for their work:

If one falls down, his friend can help him up.

But pity the man who falls and has no one to help him up!

Though one may be overpowered, two can defend themselves.

A cord of three strands is not quickly broken.[2]

## The Bath
*By Evelyn D. Hamann*

The late-afternoon sun pushed shadows from the trees and onto the concrete path as I walked between two austere brick buildings, past barred windows, to the entryway to Unit 1, North 1 of the state mental hospital. An eerie quiet filled the air. I had never before visited an institution and didn't want to today, either. But my husband, Scott, and I were legal guardians for his youngest sister, Janelle. Scott already worked long hours, so here I was. *God, I am so tired of this,* I complained silently. *I quit teaching to be home with my young sons, but now all my time is going to Janelle.*

Outwardly Janelle appeared quite normal, but she had severe mental disabilities because of a drug given to her when she was a tiny infant. Strangers were often confused by her lack of ability to comprehend, communicate, or perform simple daily tasks.

Until recently Janelle had lived with her parents, but she was thirty-five, and they weren't getting any younger. For as much joy as she brought all of us, with her childlike wonder and understanding, she needed constant supervision and care. Once, I painstakingly wrote three months' worth of dinner menus and grocery lists, all in pencil so I could revise if necessary. I posted them on the refrigerator door, proud of my unusually organized accomplishment. Later, all three pages were completely blank! Janelle, while visiting, had been left in the room alone . . . with a pencil eraser available . . . a known tool of her compulsion for neatness. Scott and I laughed until our sides ached.

Scott and his parents agreed that Janelle needed to move to a group home where her long-term needs could be met. He and I became her legal guardians, an eventuality given my in-laws' increasing health difficulties. It seemed simple at the time. Just manage her finances, take her to church, look in on her from time to time, and sit in on her care-plan development.

We found a clean, well-kept group home managed by a company that specialized in caring for adults with disabilities. Twenty-four hours a day, trained personnel aided Janelle and just three other individuals with their simple daily routines. It seemed to go well . . . that is, for the first four hours.

First came a mix-up on her state aid, then insurance, and then care issues. For weeks, every spare moment I had went to researching, calling, waiting by the phone for return calls, all without resolving anything. Worse, Janelle was *not* adjusting.

"Evelyn, please take me home. I don't like it here," she pleaded with me at each visit.

"Janelle, this *is* your new home," I reminded her over and over. Soon she began picking sores on her face, arms, and legs. Her behaviors escalated to pulling out her hair and crying with little or no provocation.

One night, just four weeks after her placement, the home supervisor called. "Evelyn, I'm . . . I . . . one of the care-givers in Janelle's house was caught taking advantage of her sexually."

Both horrified and drained by what had happened, I mechanically took action. The time I had dreamed of spending at home with my boys was soon swallowed up with, "Sawyer, take Hunter out and sit in the hall while Mom talks to the prosecutor." "Hunter, not now, Mama is talking with the doctor." Though we prosecuted the offender, we kept Janelle in the same home because she had bonded with another of the care-givers; another move might have seemed like punishment to her.

We'd no sooner cleared the court hurdles when Janelle started refusing to eat. She stayed in bed for days on end and became increasingly belligerent and physically aggressive. *How could this have happened to the sweet, helpful Janelle who even cleaned my grocery lists?* I protested in my prayers. The home kept us posted on different behavior programs they were trying, but Janelle would not cooperate.

Finally her care-givers called me, distraught. "We can't get her under control. She cannot stay here any longer, we aren't equipped for this sort of thing . . ." I rushed over, took one look at my screaming, hysterical sister-in-law, and dialed 9-1-1. That day, it took two police officers to forcibly restrain her while she shrieked angrily at the top of her lungs. I watched without emotion. *I can't help her, all my effort's done nothing, and it's keeping me from my family.*

I called through a long list, but only the state institution, where I was now visiting, would take her. Janelle didn't really fit there; convicts and severely disturbed individuals lived within the same halls. But what other choice did I have?

I pressed the intercom button. A nurse clothed in hospital green escorted me into the locked facility. "Janelle hasn't had any outbursts today," she said crisply as we walked down a barren corridor. "However, she's refusing our help. She hasn't bathed since she arrived."

I grimaced. Janelle's poor hygiene multiplied by ten days? I would be tortured by her smell. The nurse motioned to an area with a few vinyl-clad chairs and couches and said, "You wait here in the visitors' lounge and I'll get her."

As she left, I wondered how quickly I could make up some excuse, any excuse, and escape. I sat down at one end of a couch and closed my eyes to shut out the prison-like facilities. *God, I'm so tired and worn and I don't see how we can place Janelle elsewhere . . . if she would just die . . . no, I don't mean that.*

"Evelyn?" It was the voice of a timid, unsure child . . . my sister-in-law. Her eyes peeked at me through her long, black, greasy and uncombed hair; was that relief at seeing me? The borrowed clothing she wore was inside out, way too big for her.

Repulsed, I reminded myself, *It's not my fault she's such a mess. Or that she's here. She could have cooperated at the home.* Her smell already permeated the room, a mixture of body odor and fecal matter. I winced, wanting to hold my nose. After a pause, I said, "Yes, Janelle. I came to see you."

"Evelyn, would you please pray with me?" Startled, I studied her face. Janelle often parroted sayings from movies, cartoons, or prior conversations without understanding. This time her eyes pleaded with me. I glanced down, a bit ashamed.

"Sure, Janelle. Come sit by me." Timidly, she reached out her hands to mine. Before I could start, she began. "Jesus, I need you. Please help me to love and not be so angry." Now I was alert. *Angry? That's* my *problem, too.* "And, Jesus, thank you for Evelyn and Scott and my Mommy and Daddy. I love them so. They are always there for me. Please keep them safe. Let them know how much I love them. Amen."

A large lump filled my throat. I had never heard her speak so clearly, with so much understanding. I opened my eyes. How pale her slender fingers appeared as they gently lay in my hands. A tear fell from her cheek. I mumbled a few closing words, "Lord, Janelle is your precious child and our precious sister." *How had I forgotten that?* "Help us all today. . . ."

When we finished I looked up at her and asked, "Janelle, would you like me to bathe you and help brush your teeth?" The words sprang from my mouth before I could stop them. Bathe her? How many times had I told my mother-in-law that I would never, ever, feel comfortable bathing a woman almost as old as I was? *Surely she'll refuse, just as the nurse reported,* I reassured myself. But Janelle slowly pulled aside the hair hanging in her eyes and nodded, with a childlike look of innocence, yes.

I gathered the needed supplies. *Go figure,* I thought. *Angry as I am, I'm agreeing to do this?* But somehow I felt soiled, too, with my resentment and anger. *God, I don't know what you are going to do with me, but I don't want to be like this anymore. Please change me.*

I helped Janelle disrobe, carefully placing her soiled garments far from the clean ones I had found. She managed to get into the tub while I filled a pitcher with warm water. "Close your eyes, honey. This is going to feel mighty good," I said, as if speaking to my boys.

She compliantly let me soap, scrub, and rinse first her hair, then her body. We began to joke and laugh as the rinses and splashes got me almost as wet as she was. As the layers of oil, odor, and grime fell away from her, my own bitterness and exhaustion loosened their grip as well. *Lord,* I prayed, *I need your eyes and your love to see Janelle as you do.*

I finished helping her dress and brushed her teeth. Janelle sat quietly before me in the chair while I carefully and gently combed out each hair tangle. No screaming, no crying. My heart was quiet as well. No bitter thoughts or anger. As I looked ahead in the mirror, I saw a clean, sweet, scared little three-year-old housed in a woman's body, who longed to be loved and protected. Then I looked up and saw myself. I saw something I hadn't seen in quite some time—a smile, one that permeated into my heart. I liked what I saw on both counts.

I walked down the path to my car. An overly large, bright orange harvest moon had overtaken the sun for its place in the sky, kind of like the change of heart I felt inside. *"Don't do this alone,"* God seemed to say.

That had been my problem. Even though I'd prayed, I'd also played the martyr, trying to solve Janelle's problems alone, totally losing sight of my main responsibility—and heart's desire—of making sure Janelle knows she's loved by us and by God.

––––––––

*Evelyn spoke with her husband that night, and later that week they both met with Scott's parents. They each took on certain responsibilities, agreeing to confer and pray with one another regarding Janelle's needs.*

*Almost immediately, things started to change. A federal investigator was named on Janelle's behalf because of the mistreatment she had received. Because of this, she was moved into a loving, secure environment better suited to her special needs. She was remarkably provided with training for personal, social, and professional needs . . . something previously denied time and time again.*

*It took a while, but the Janelle they once knew—the "little girl"—is back. She again delights them with her smiles and causes them to laugh at her antics. Evelyn says, "God's love has cleansed both her and me."*

## Listening
### By Fred Scaife

Challenges bring out the best in me. At my company, the more messed up a department was, the more likely I'd be asked to take over. My new assignment? Managing Director of our international data centers in Brussels, Belgium, overseeing operations in eighteen countries. My orders? To get financials under control and cut customer complaints.

I'd once spent three years in Belgium, so I knew I fit into the business culture. I took one advance trip before moving, to pick out a house for my family and meet my predecessor. I didn't see a reason to meet with anyone else. They'd be on board with my strategies soon enough.

That first morning I looked around my new office with its typical office furniture and lovely view out the window. I hung up my coat, unpacked my briefcase, and set out pictures of my wife and children.

First, I would meet all my managers. Then I'd give a speech outlining changes to be made, and my new staff would get to work. That was the corporate expectation, providing the vision and the road map.

Hans, the most senior manager, was at the top of my list. I knocked politely on his door. A slender, sandy-haired man perhaps ten years younger than me looked up, frowned, and muttered, "Come in."

His office had a professional air, the only clutter being a few neat stacks of papers. Framed diplomas and awards showed he was well qualified and apparently effective at what he did. I extended my hand to shake his, but Hans ignored it. I could feel my face reddening, but I introduced myself and added, "From all I've heard, you are vital to this office."

He shrugged. I tried again. "Are there any urgent matters for the day?"

He answered in flawless English, "Everything is urgent, no one listens, so nothing will get done."

*His attitude may be half of what's wrong here,* I thought, then said aloud, "Well, I'll be outlining my plans this afternoon."

"You've figured out how to solve our problems in a day?" Hans snapped. Then he added, softly, "I should have had your job." He nervously set aside the document he was reading and reached for another.

No one talked to me that way! I thought about firing him on the spot but decided to meet all the managers before deciding how many heads would roll.

But as I introduced myself to the other managers, my stomach sank. Hans was just the tip of the iceberg! Not one of them suggested meeting for lunch. No one even welcomed me! Instead, they snarled, whined, and snapped comments like, "We don't have authority to do that." "Can't be done." "Why try when the other departments won't?"

I fled back to my office, less sure of myself than I had been since my first day of kindergarten. I had a full-fledged mutiny on my hands. What was more, I had no idea how to squelch it. All my other tough assignments had been solved through new software designs, applications, or training, my specialty. How would I fix people?

Just then Nicole, my new office manager, came in with business cards for me. "Do you drink coffee?" she asked.

Thinking it might clear my head, I said, "Let's have a cup together. Show me where the pot is."

I followed her through the maze of offices to a small, quiet break room. By the time we arrived, she'd asked about my family, my preference for cream or sugar, and whether I missed baseball already.

As we sat down, Nicole asked, "What will you need for this afternoon?" She asked other questions about how I liked to run things. As I answered, she jotted a few notes on a pad she'd brought along. At the end, she said, "I'll get right on the following items," and proceeded to list out several things she planned to do for me, many of which I hadn't mentioned. I thought, *What a good listener . . . she could probably run this place!*

Then I remembered the words Hans had spoken, *"No one listens."* I hadn't planned to, either. No, I was all set to tell them exactly what I wanted them to do. When was the last time I'd sat still and listened to anyone?

I went back to my office and closed the door, the word *listen* echoing over and over in my head. As I stared out the window, the first thought that came to me was, *What does God want you to do?* I almost snorted. I was supposed to run my office while God ran everything else. But perhaps . . . of course God knew about managing people. What if I listened to God? I pulled out a note pad and pencil, determined to imitate Nicole.

As I stilled my thoughts, waiting for the wisdom I lacked, I recalled what Jesus said, *"Whoever wants to become great among you must be your servant."* [3] Me, be a servant to this office? How?

A polite knock interrupted my thoughts as Nicole popped in with an envelope marked "Urgent." The brief memo inside read, "Effective immediately, I hereby resign my position as operations manager . . . Hans." Maybe I could start serving by listening to this angry, yet talented, man. I asked Nicole to summon him.

Hans came in and stood in front of my desk without looking at me. I said, "I guess I shouldn't be surprised at your memo. Please sit down."

As he slouched into a chair, I added, "I cancelled this afternoon's meeting. In its place, what if next week you and the rest of the managers present to me on what is and isn't working here?"

Hans was quiet for the longest time, but I kept my mouth shut. Finally he looked up and spoke. "Do you mean you'll hear us out?"

"Right." I fought my natural impulse to control and instead said, "How should the meeting go?"

"Well, past meetings usually ended in shouts. . . ." Hans shared how my predecessor had spent more time out of the office than in it. The managers had had to fend for themselves, making the atmosphere more like a boxing arena than an office. Then he suggested a meeting format that seemed to ensure that everyone would be heard.

As Hans stood up, I said, "Before you go, would you mind if I sat on your memo for a while?"

Hans mumbled, "If you think that's best," and left.

Over the next several days, I stilled my soul each morning at my desk, then prayed that I'd continue to listen. For the meeting to succeed, I knew

I had to do two things: keep my mouth shut, and support their ideas by ensuring action.

The way Hans drew everyone together at the meeting took me by surprise. He spoke first. As he invited the others to openly question his ideas, everyone began to relax. By the time sandwiches were delivered for lunch, the managers were competing over which department had confessed to the longest list of weaknesses. By the end of the day, the once-demoralized managers were excited about the list of action items they'd compiled. Further, their plan was more targeted and thorough than any I could have made.

Within minutes of our adjournment, Hans popped his head into my office. "Uh, could I have that resignation letter back?" For the first time we shook hands.

Within days of the meeting, the most common sound in the office was laughter. Within six months we were making our financial goals. Within the year, our customer service rating rose from terrible to very good.

That was the end of Fred, the corporate top-down leader. In the years that followed, as I moved on to Norway and England, then to my own business, I never again assumed I had all the answers. Instead, I stop, still my soul, listening first to God and then to my managers, including my office manager, of course!

————

*Fred, now retired, mentors the leadership team of Daystar University in Nairobi, Kenya. Since 1999, he and his wife, Elsie, now in their mid-seventies, have spent about half of their time in Kenya.*

*Daystar University is a full-fledged accredited liberal arts school of 2,200 students from nineteen different African countries. Fred also consults on the organization's strategic planning and application of information systems and technology. Fred visited the school as part of a short visit to Africa with his church. When they learned of his technology background, they invited him to work with them.*

*He says, "Never in my life have I felt such fulfillment, doing work that I love and knowing that my knowledge is needed. I firmly believe God led me to this work and guides me day by day in doing it."*

## Tongue-Tied

*By Susan Whitehead*

"Hi, Susan," a cheery voice greeted me as I answered the phone. It was Debbie, a young woman I had mentored for several years. "Debbie! I've been thinking about you," I answered.

"Really? You've been on my mind, too. I want to ask you something, but please don't answer right away. Just listen, and promise to pray about it. Okay?"

"Sure," I said.

Debbie caught me up on her progress toward establishing a group called MOPS (Mothers of Preschoolers) in our church. Fall was fast approaching and the leadership team was pretty much in place, except for one position. "Here's where I see you, as our 'Mentor Mom.'"

I loved it! Our three adult children all lived at least a thousand miles from us. Other than a few visits a year, our relationships and communication were frustratingly long distance. I'd enjoyed mentoring several young women like Debbie and had been praying that the Lord would enlarge that ministry. God was about to answer my prayer!

"What's the job description?" I asked, trying not to sound too eager, but more in control, the way I thought a potential Mentor Mom might sound.

"Just to be you," she answered cheerily. "Just be there for us, be an encourager, support the steering committee." She continued, running through a short list of duties. "And you'd give a forty-five-minute teaching once or twice a month to the group."

My brain froze into thousands of tiny icy needles. Forty-five minutes standing up on a platform before a microphone, offering wisdom to sixty-five young women? About ten years ago our pastor sent a note asking me to present one of Jesus' seven last words at a Good Friday service. Horrified, I asked him if he had prayed about it. He assured me he had, and that the talk would only be five to ten minutes. With overwhelming dread I agreed. That night, robed appropriately in black, I sat on the raised altar area with six others, certain my heart could not maintain its furious pounding and, in a very few minutes, I would die, right there in front of the congregation.

"No, I'm sorry," I quickly answered, my heart again pounding so hard

I could scarcely hold the receiver. This was one opportunity I didn't need to think about—or bother God about, either. After my single past experience I kindly promised myself that NEVER AGAIN would I go through that. This sow's ear was never going to be a silk purse, and that was that.

But after I hung up I felt sadly wistful. So close, and yet so far. A dream for someone; a nightmare for me. No, my Creator knows what I can and can't do . . . and this particular creation does not have a gift for public speaking! I envisioned myself in front of a microphone, stuttering, trembling, literally dying of fright in front of all those young women. Debbie needed to find a Mentor Mom with a different set of gifts!

I watched from the sidelines during the next year as the MOPS group flourished, catching snippets of conversation and reading updates and announcements in the church bulletin. More than once I regretted that I could not be part of it, yet praised God that I wasn't, glad that they had found someone better suited to help the group.

But late in the spring, my phone rang. Again Debbie said, "I want to ask you something. I don't want you to answer right away. Just listen, and promise to pray about it. Okay?"

"I'm listening, Debbie."

"If we got speakers to come in, instead of asking you to do the teaching, would you pray about being our Mentor Mom?"

The word *yes* flew from my mouth instantly! Now my heart pounded with excitement, not panic. God was so good, answering prayers I hadn't even prayed!

As the planning team met for the coming year, my joy at being part of the ministry grew. The program came together amazingly well. I felt vaguely guilty as the steering committee struggled to line up speakers for the year. When the discussion turned to setting the speaker fees, I stared at my lap in slight embarrassment.

At one of the final meetings, we learned that a speaker had cancelled. I squirmed as usual but was broadsided by the committee member's next request. "Susan, we need you to please fill in just this once. The topic is 'Intimacy After Children Arrive.' You can do it! It doesn't have to be a big deal. Please?"

I forced myself to think rationally. *I'm trapped! My role is to help this group in every way possible. I can't start whimpering about my lack of equipment, my comfort zone, my desire to sleep at night. My back's to the wall. Lord, what did you tell Moses? "Certainly I will be with you."*[4] I nodded as sheer terror took control.

My husband walked in the door to a full-blown crisis standing before him.

"Remember? I said 'NO.' Because I can't! I just can't. . . . But now, this time, and what could I say? I'm supposed to help. They don't have any idea. . . ."

When he wandered through the maze of my rambling, disconnected story, he was as sympathetic as he could be without being able to really understand. He's one of God's creations who *does* possess a gift for public speaking. He loves it. He is also a problem-solver.

"Do you want me to give the talk for you?" A vision, unbidden, filled my mind: my husband standing on that platform discussing intimacy in marriage before sixty-five young women!

"No, no," I murmured, finally smiling.

"Well, then, how can I help?"

I sadly just shook my head. Short of a surgical transplant of confidence, I couldn't think of a single way.

"Tell you what," he said, trying again, "you can put down what you want to say as a wife mentor, and write in parts for a husband mentor. We could take turns."

Hope leapt up. Yes! He could hold my hand as we walked up so I wouldn't fall. They would look at him and not me. If I were struck dumb, he could fill in. Plus, our teaching would be so different that no one would compare me to the other speakers.

Hmmm, with my husband . . . all of a sudden, ideas danced through my mind. Dare I confess that this was turning out to be the tiniest bit of fun? Was this possible?

Yes, my heart pounded so hard that morning that I changed what I was wearing so the huge beats would not be observed. Yes, despite my husband's presence, I couldn't camouflage my violently shaking hands, nor remove the quiver from my voice. Yes, I barely looked at anyone in the audience. But yes, I made it!

Forty-five minutes later, as we stepped down from the platform, my feet seemed to glide over the floor. The meeting moved on, but not before I noticed hands reaching for tissues to dab at eyes. Oh my.

As I sat there, my heart still pounding, I marveled at how God did not give up on me, but opened yet another door to this ministry after I had so arrogantly slammed the first one shut. *"Certainly I will be with you. . . ."*

I had always been impatient with Moses. After all, with God standing right there in front of him in the form of that proverbial burning bush, Moses had the audacity to say "No." Hmmmm.

———————

*Susan was able to continue on her own (with occasional help from her friend, the public speaker) to give more teachings. She was never cool, calm, and collected, but she lived through the experiences with God, who says, "Certainly I will be with you," and who continues reaching down to grasp her little, shaky hand.*

## KEY: The path before you may require the gifts of those around you.

When we think we need to act on God's callings alone, several traps lie in wait.

*Martyrdom.* Paul tells us, "Each of you should look not only to your own interests, but also to the interests of others."[5] It doesn't say, "instead" but "also." If a task begins to overwhelm your physical, mental, or spiritual resources, ask for help. A good test for this is to ask yourself whether there is any end to your burdens in sight.

*Half a job.* The writer of Ecclesiastes reminds us that, "Two are better than one, because they have a good return for their work."[6] Often, more gets done—or the quality of work goes up—when teams form. People sometimes ask me, "How can you work with a coauthor? Isn't writing a solitary pursuit?" I tell them of writing *Find Your Fit*, our teen version of *LifeKeys*. I could have written it myself, especially since I taught teens in Sunday school for years, but instead I teamed with Kevin Johnson. Not only had he written several books for teens, but he'd been a youth pastor for three hundred adolescents. I welcomed his experience rather than working to get it myself!

*Work left undone.* If you avoid a task, certain that God can't be calling you because you don't have the gifts, something may be left undone. Instead, share your thoughts. You might find a willing partner who's the key to making it happen.

The first time that Jesus sent His disciples out in ministry, He sent them out two by two, not each alone.[7] If you can't fathom how God could possibly think you capable of some task—as small as a single speech or as big as changing an office—before you say, "Send someone else," ask, "Is someone going to help me?"

*Moses and Aaron*
*Joshua and Caleb*
*Ruth and Naomi*
*Shadrach, Meshach, and Abednego*
*Peter and John*
*Paul and Silas*
*Priscilla and Aquila*
*Help me remember that two are often better than one, Lord. Amen.*

---

[1]Exodus 18:13
[2]Ecclesiastes 4:9–10, 12
[3]Matthew 20:26
[4]Exodus 3:12 NASB
[5]Philippians 2:4
[6]Ecclesiastes 4:9
[7]Mark 6:7

# 9

# If the Going Gets Tough, Did I Make a Wrong Turn?

**Key: Jesus' promise was twofold: "In this world you will have trouble. But take heart! I have overcome the world."[1]**

*Much of Paul's first missionary journey with Barnabas was grim. First, the leaders in Pisidian Antioch banished them from the region. Then they barely escaped stoning in Iconium.*

*They fled twenty miles to Lystra. When Paul healed a lame man, the townspeople declared that Barnabas was the Greek god Zeus and Paul, Hermes. Even as Paul and Barnabas tried to describe the one true God, men from Antioch and Iconium, who had followed them, wooed the crowd, convincing them to stone Paul.*

*Picture an angry mob, yelling and shouting as they pushed and shoved him toward the city gates. The designated witnesses threw the first stones. Others joined in, the landscape providing an endless arsenal. Surely at first Paul bravely faced his accusers, perhaps even remembering the death of the apostle Stephen when he stood as witness. As the stones hailed down, he would have faltered, sunk to his knees, succumbed.*

*Thinking he was dead, his accusers dragged him outside the city.*

*But Paul lived. The Bible tells us that the next day he and Barnabas headed for Derbe, this time fleeing over sixty miles from their troubles. What did they talk about as they walked?*

———

Barnabas glanced back across the rocky fields they'd traversed. He wished they could quicken their step, get out of the open, in case they were again being followed. Paul, though, couldn't walk any faster. *But he's walking, thanks be to God,* he reminded himself. He squeezed his eyes shut, trying to erase the image of Paul sprawled in the dust, bruised, bleeding, lifelessly still.

Paul stumbled slightly and reached out for Barnabas's arm. "We'll get there . . . at this pace just an extra day."

"Two, I think . . . but I have plenty of bread for us."

"Ah, the people of Lystra were so kind—"

"Paul, they nearly *killed* you!"

Paul shrugged. "It's for the best. People should know their lives might be at stake before they follow Jesus. In a few weeks, when we return to Lystra, they'll know that our mission is more important than our lives."

Barnabas glanced nervously over his shoulder again. "A few weeks? That's not enough time for things to cool down. I want to go back, thank those who helped us escape, but our enemies have long, long memories."

Paul halted, then slowly slid his hands down the front of his legs, as if trying to ease his back. "Let's rest for a second," he murmured, gesturing toward a low stone fence.

Barnabas strode ahead, quickly folding his extra cloak into a pillow for Paul to sit on. He reached out his arm to steady his companion as Paul painfully seated himself. Slowly, Paul stretched out one foot, then the other, then closed his eyes. *Go back?* Barnabas asked himself. *He'd be throwing his life away.*

The two sat quietly for a moment. Barnabas stared at the ground. Paul looked over at him, then reached down and picked up two stones, one as round and smooth as a bird's egg, the other with a razor-sharp edge, as if it had been chiseled to form an ax head. He held one in each hand, feeling their heft as he spoke.

"Either of these, aimed well, could kill me. This one, though," he murmured, holding out the jagged-edged stone, "looks more lethal. It's the same with the places we go. Time and again the Holy Spirit has warned me that prison—or worse—waits for me in the next town. But still, ways open up! Antioch, Iconium, Lystra . . . despite our problems we managed to tell people about Jesus. And some believed! The faster we visit them again, the less of a chance that their fears about our fates will overcome their newly born beliefs."

Barnabas took the stone from Paul's hand and tested its sharpness with his finger. "I understand. We either keep running headfirst into danger or keep silent—trouble is simply a given."

Paul nodded vigorously. "We can't take obstacles as signs to stop. Think of the size of the crowds we attracted in Antioch. Of course we angered some of the leaders. Of course they came after us. But when we return, our message so clearly more important to us than our lives, they'll see how God enables us to do far more than we could ever imagine doing on our own."

"And your vision of what we can do is far bigger than mine," Barnabas said as he gently dropped the rock to the ground beside their bundle of provisions. "Onward!"

———

*When the going gets tough, it's only natural to wonder whether we did something wrong or somehow got off the path God intended for us to follow. Jesus, though, promised us that life would be full of hardships. Paul went so far as to rejoice in those hardships, believing that they made his testimony even stronger. It seems as if Paul trained himself to look for the positive side of every trouble.*

*However, Paul did leave Lystra after the stoning. His view of hardship didn't extend to foolhardiness. He and Barnabas journeyed to Derbe, where many became disciples through their preaching. Then they returned to Lystra, Iconium, and Antioch, telling the new Christians in those towns, "We must go through many hardships to enter the kingdom of God." [2]*

*In the following stories you'll read about troubles that seem overwhelming, yet Jesus fulfilled His promise of helping each person take heart. God's presence reassured them that they were on the right path, no matter how rocky the terrain.*

I delight in weaknesses, in insults, in hardships, in persecutions, in difficulties. For when I am weak, then I am strong. [3]

## Not on Our Own
### By Barbara Marshak

A literal mountain of snow loomed across the full width of my driveway. Somehow the snowplow had managed to dump all the excess snow in my driveway as it rounded the curve where the street widened. Standing alone in the dark, I stared at the task before me, doubting that my solitary shovel could handle the massive job.

I took a deep breath and jabbed the shovel into the hard, crusty mound, tossing the heavy snow to the side, one shovelful at a time. Again and again, like a robot, jab and toss, jab and toss. Like most Minnesota communities, ordinances required that no vehicles could be left on the streets overnight. My car was still parked a precarious distance away from the buried curb, so I had no choice but to keep at it.

I had purchased the older, story-and-a-half Tudor the previous August. Recently divorced, I discovered I qualified for a federal home loan and had quickly selected the gray house at 818 SW Second Street to call my own. The loan officer had been more than a little reluctant to let me—a single mom—proceed, even though I met the stringent guidelines. To me the house had *character*, not concerns. And even more importantly, it was only a few blocks from my daughters' school—doubly perfect, since my new job was in the same building. Altogether, I felt it was another confirmation of God's guiding hand throughout this transitional year.

To be honest, I'd only recently committed my life to God, and I was new at listening for direction from above. I had all the confidence in the world that I could handle the surface issues, but I wasn't quite as sure about potential structural problems like the roof—one of the points the loan administrator had bluntly pointed out. Now I was trying to cope with the first blizzard of the year, and judging by the pile of snow, Mother Nature was the winner and I was the loser. *God, did I rush ahead without you?*

We had always rented throughout our ten-year marriage, so I'd felt a strong need to put down roots and have a real home for my daughters and me. As soon as we moved in I began painting and decorating the interior. Karli, eight, and Emily, five, asked to share the big bedroom upstairs, and even assisted me in hanging a coordinating border. We picked a cheery yellow for the spare bedroom and turned that into their playroom.

The dining room seemed too formal, so I added a small table in the roomy kitchen, just right for the three of us. Part of the main floor became my sewing room, handy for working on quilts. The girls made friends in the neighborhood and loved having sleep-overs, dragging their beloved blankies up and down the tree-lined blocks. All in all, the days were going rather smoothly with our work and school schedules—until Mt. Everest hit. Maybe I'd been playing home decorator rather than homeowner.

*What if something does happen to the roof?* I wondered, remembering the loan officer's cynical comments. I glanced at the smoke coming out of the chimney, the lights shining in the windows. After a full day at work I wanted to be inside, snuggled with Karli and Emily on the couch.

Just then I heard a banging on the living room window. Both girls waved at me. I trudged toward the house, my toes already numb. "What?" I yelled, wiping my dripping nose with my frozen glove.

"We're hungry!" they cried from inside.

"Just wait," I yelled back. "I'm not done yet!" Not done—my shoulders and back were killing me and I had hardly made a dent!

I looked up at the girls, both crying, their noses pressed up against the frosted glass, and then at the driveway still full of snow. Overwhelmed by it all, I started crying myself. Angrily I threw the shovel at the snowbank, wiped my own tears from my icy cheeks, and headed inside.

We sat at our little table, quietly sipping hot soup while the ominous wind continued to howl outside. I settled the girls on the couch in their pajamas before I plunged outside for another round.

But a neighbor from across the street was making incredible progress with his snowblower on my driveway. A wave of relief swept over me as I waved a thank-you to him and began shoveling the sidewalk with renewed energy.

Later that night, sporting sore muscles, I climbed into bed and turned on the little lamp, cherishing this quiet, uninterrupted time in my day. As usual, I began with my daily devotional and corresponding Scripture before journaling my thoughts. I picked up my pen, toes still tingling, ready to record my self-pitying feelings from earlier in the evening.

Before I started writing, however, I began scanning through the previous days and weeks. Page after page, I read through my urgent concerns of the past. None of them were a bother anymore. Much like my mountain of snow, each obstacle had somehow been resolved. *You may be a single parent,* the pages seemed to say, *but you're not alone in this.* You might say that God sent an angel with a snowblower to remind me.

Maybe I couldn't calm a winter storm, but I could see God had shoveled a distinct path through another trying circumstance, sustaining me once again. I had no guarantee that the roof wouldn't leak or the foundation wouldn't crack, but God was the true cornerstone of our lives. I simply needed to elevate my faith to trust God, regardless of the unknowns.

––––––––––

*Barbara's years as a single parent hold a special place in her heart. It was a time when God became a real and viable part of her daily life as she learned to trust and depend on her Lord. Thankfully, that lesson has proven valuable through many more decisions in her life. Today, Barbara and her husband have a blended family of six children, five of whom are grown. She continually strives to raise her faith to trust God to move around that next corner, whatever that may be.*

## Welcome to the Dawn
*By Suzanne P. Campbell*

It was four A.M. on a May morning and I was restless, unable to sleep. I arose from bed and went out to my condo balcony, five stories above the silent street. It had rained for hours; the air was moist and still. I wrapped an old quilt around me and sat on the porch glider, a pillow under my bare feet to cushion them from the cold concrete floor. Rocking gently, I listened to scattered droplets fall from the water-laden maple tree beneath the balcony railing.

The last eighteen months had been discouraging. Failed knee surgery had left me unable to bend or move my right leg without pain. My income was substantially reduced while medical expenses had increased. I had prayed before deciding to have the surgery. Did I fail to sense God's will? Why had I spent months suffering with no end in sight? Had God abandoned me?

For hours I chased these questions like elusive squirrels in my head, turning more and more inward. Myself, my needs, my hurt filled my being. Did this kind of life have any purpose?

At a writing conference, just before my surgery, an editor had suggested that I develop a book proposal about my career as a counselor and submit it to him. He emphasized his excitement about it. A book! I immediately began to gather and organize materials, setting a deadline for completing the proposal in November. I didn't know, though, that I'd face knee surgery in October. Book proposals are complex and time consuming; they also do not produce immediate income. Another dream deferred; I had to spend my energy more practically.

I sighed, breathing in the damp night air as my mind catalogued the treasured activities my knee problems had curtailed. I spent less time with friends, missed church services, limited my hours for volunteering, and couldn't bear the thought of the long car trips I loved.

My daughter, Joy, and her new husband, Kyle, had bought their first home in Lansing, two states away. Since Joy's college years in Michigan, I had made the trip there several times. I loved to drive, hitting the road with the company of an audio book or just singing along with my favorite tapes. Joy and Kyle had been in their home for almost two years. *If only I'd visited before the surgery,* I sighed. Joy had sent pictures, but we both knew it wasn't the same as a visit. How could I go, though, when just getting up, showering. and dressing exhausted me on some days?

Filled with despair, I cried out to the Lord, "Help me! My life has no purpose. How did I move so far from your will?" The air remained damp and still as I rocked slowly, overwhelmed by the pain that ruled me.

Yet in the quiet moments that followed my prayer, I sensed a message, *"I'm here. I never left your side, but if you are filled with the power of pain, then there is no room for me. Release your pain to my care."*

Relief rushed through me, joy at God's presence. But release my pain? How could I do that when my slightest movement reminded me of my problems? I'd prayed for God to take it away, but not really for help in living with it . . . was that why the pain controlled me so? I didn't know how to do what God was asking.

"Lord," I prayed, "I want to give my pain into your hands, please help me. I don't want to bear it by myself anymore. And . . . forgive me for letting it rule my life. Fill me instead with your Spirit."

Gradually, as I rocked and prayed, my spirits lightened. I looked up. The sky had cleared and I could see a scattering of stars hidden, then revealed, from pockets in the clouds. God seemed to say, *"See how much bigger your world is, the world beyond your pain?"* Suddenly, my thoughts whirled with prayer requests from friends and family. I had been brushing them off because I had nothing left to give.

Between the night and the morning I spent a joyous time "standing in the gap" for people I loved. I prayed for my friend whose daughter had just announced she was pregnant. Unmarried, she wanted her mom to help her decide what to do. And my nephew Peter—I needed to pray for his upcoming mission trip to India. Other faces and concerns came to mind.

When I finished, from the trees beneath me the first bird offered its welcome to the dawn. On this silent morning, the still, small voice of God spoke to me through its song, celebrating my re-creation as a person with purpose.

Weeks have passed and my life *is* changed. As I sit on the balcony, I can smell the pungent tang of a potted rosemary bush mixed with the lighter scents of roses and lemon thyme. My body still aches, but I no longer allow it to rule my thoughts. I do what I can and accept the bad days as temporary setbacks.

I resumed a volunteer job as a phone counselor after making arrangements to park my car right outside, rather than walking half a mile from the designated lot. When my nephew Tim's birthday arrived, I proposed a family dinner at my home. No stairs. If I am scheduled to review a play for the local newspaper I ice my knee, put on a brace for support, and head out the door.

On my birthday I received a surprise plane ticket to Michigan from my daughter and son-in-law. At first I hesitated, but my son, Mike, said, "Mom, just go. I'll drive you to the airport and pick you up when you get home. It'll be fine."

My time in Lansing was wonderful. I explored Joy and Kyle's new home, enjoyed my son-in-law's homemade gourmet pancakes, and visited Joy's office on the university campus.

As I told my prayer group at church recently, "The pain has not changed, but God has changed me." Truly, a new day in my life has dawned.

––––––––

*Sue is currently planning to have her knee surgery redone. Meanwhile, her temporary disability has given her new insights about living as a Christian. "God doesn't promise that we will live without pain, but rather to be with us in our pain. Recently I felt led to Isaiah 40:31 (NRSV), 'but those who wait on the Lord shall renew their strength; they shall mount up with wings like eagles, they shall run and not be weary, they shall walk and not faint.' How encouraging!"*

## Safe in God's Loving Arms
*By Julia Nicole* [4]

I wasn't a cheerleader, or head of student council, or first chair in band. Nothing in my little world of school or circle of friends counteracted my family's message that I was worthless.

An after-school moment, typical yet painful, stands out. I'd just walked in the door from school and planned to grab a glass of milk before retreating to my room to tackle homework. But before I could hide, my brother filled the kitchen doorway, stared at me for a moment, then shook his head. "God, you're ugly," he spat, wrinkling his face in disgust as he walked away.

My eyes burned with tears I refused to release. Guarding my wounded heart, I escaped to my room and crawled inside myself.

There, unconditional love and acceptance dwelled, just as God had promised me years before. I was too young to understand the words when I first understood God's message. I remember the moment clearly.

My father sat in a large, dark green overstuffed chair near the front door and I on the floor at his feet. The windows and inside front door were open. It was quite warm. The living room lights were on, yet my older brothers and I had not been sent off to bed, so it must have been an early fall evening. I wore only my diaper, plastic pants, and undershirt. I was just a toddler.

My father and brothers had their eyes fixed on the television. My eyes, however, were on my father's lap. I wanted him to touch me, pick me up, hold me. I wanted to feel the love and security of my father's arms around me. I patted his leg and tugged on his pants—no response. Babbling in the language of a toddler, I tried to communicate my desire—still no response. Finally I stuck out my tongue and gave him a "raspberry."

That got my father's attention, all right. He snatched me up, hauled me off to the bedroom, and slammed me in my crib. Without a word, he walked out, leaving me alone in the dark.

It all happened so quickly. This wasn't what I wanted. His harsh, silent response frightened me. My wails filled the house. Reappearing at the bedroom door, my father shouted angrily, "Shut up! Just shut up! It's your own fault!" Then he was gone.

Though only a toddler, I understood. I told myself, *It was wrong to want him to hold you. You are bad.*

Terrified, I swallowed my tears and gasped for breath. The lights from the living room shone down the hall. I heard my brothers talking and laughing together. My heart was crushed by the isolation. Sitting in the dark, staring through the bars of my crib, I made a desperate attempt to float out of myself and away from the overwhelming hurt.

Then in the darkness I felt a new presence that seemed to lift my fears and replace them with love. Sitting quietly, enveloped in the safety of this love, the tears dried from my eyes and my heart heard a promise: *"I will never leave you. Remember, I am always with you."* That presence I later recognized as God.

The memory of that night came back again and again during adolescence as I suffered my family's abuse, guarding my heart until I could move out on my own. I *knew* the worst of life was behind me. Each day I gave thanks for the image of God holding me, teaching me where my real security lies.

Still, I fought with feelings that I was of no value, of no real worth. In my battle to gain my family's respect, I often set impossible standards for myself. As an adult, when I failed to meet yet another unreachable goal, I tailspinned into self-criticisms: *You should never . . . You should always . . . You are so stupid! You can't do anything right!* Eventually, my mind grew dizzy with accusations and shut down. Failure chased me back inside myself, re-creating the security of my crib until the reassurance found in God's loving arms convinced me to emerge and try again.

My need to retreat reinforced my feelings of worthlessness and immaturity and yet helped me recover. Each time I seemed a bit more confident that I was of value. Finally I met a man who seemed healthy, safe. We even talked of marriage. One phone call shattered my false security.

"Is there something you need to tell me?" he asked.

"What do you mean?"

"How could you do something so cruel? Do you have any idea how much hurt you've caused?" He wouldn't tell me what I'd been accused of. But he ordered, "Don't ever do that to anyone again!" The line clicked dead, as did our relationship.

As the reality of his rejection set in I crumpled into a chair, my face in my hands, and sobbed. Feelings of worthlessness flared like wildfire. Through the night my heart cried out over and over, *How could you be so foolish? How could you let yourself believe any man would ever love you?*

This time I couldn't retreat. When morning came, work and other obligations forced me to shower, to dress, to get in my car. As I gripped the steering wheel, fresh grief seared my heart, pangs of unjust rejection. *Lord, I can't do this, I need you,* I prayed as tears streaked my face.

Slowly, imperceptibly at first, a gentle peace began to ease my pain, then spread like a cool, healing salve. *"Julia,"* God's presence spoke, *"I am with you wherever you are. You don't need to hide from the world to find me."*

God *was* with me, right there in the car. While I still grieved for a long time over that painful loss of love and respect, I kept moving forward, able to pray, *God I need your presence here, where I am.*

I shudder to think where despair might have driven me, as an adolescent or an adult, without the image of God holding me, protecting me from self-hatred and moving me into a future of fulfilling work for others. I'd love to think that at this point in my life the worst is over—who wouldn't? But I don't know what is ahead for me. Only God knows that. What I *do* know is that whatever happens, wherever I am, I can count on God's promise to be with me always. God's loving arms will hold me and remind me, once again, of my true source of security.

———

*This is the first time Julia, a freelance writer, has put into print any of the nightmare of abuse she suffered as a child. While she still doesn't feel ready to share her identity, she hopes this story will help others reach out and find God's love, no matter how difficult their circumstances.*

**KEY: Jesus' promise was twofold: "In this world you will have trouble. But take heart! I have overcome the world."**

All of us face trouble in life. Jesus made that clear. This side of heaven, sickness, misunderstandings, accidents, and the fallout from evil mean that grief, anger, frustration, and even terror come to us all.

Still, when dark times come, our first inclination is to think, *Did I do something wrong? God, are you punishing me?* Sometimes the answer is, *"No, this is just part of life."*

Think of all the trouble Paul and Barnabas encountered at Lystra. Yet later in Antioch, Paul "reported all that God had done through them and how he had opened the door of faith to the Gentiles."[5] Years later, Paul described his reasons for staying in Ephesus, "because a great door for effective work has opened to me, and there are many who oppose me."[6] He mentions open doors and enemy opposition in the same sentence. We will have trouble, yet take heart!

However, it is worth asking, Is your situation the result of poor choices in the past? Sometimes we do need to ask for forgiveness or admit a mistake so we can get back on track. And sometimes we have to live with the consequences of what we ate, how we treated a neighbor, who we associated with, where we went.

Take time to still your soul, to hear what God might be saying. It can be so tough to remember that God is still there, that God is sovereign. Yet as Barb and Suzanne and Julia all showed, even the darkness is brighter when you keep your eyes on God.

*The darkness chokes off my faith, God.*
*I struggle to catch even a glimmer of you*
> *Did I miss your plan?*
>> *Is this what I deserve?*
*Or . . . is this life? And if so . . .*
*grasp my heart until I feel your presence*
*and can once again move forward. Amen.*

---

[1] John 16:33
[2] Acts 14:22
[3] 2 Corinthians 12:10
[4] Names have been changed.
[5] Acts 14:27
[6] 1 Corinthians 16:8

# 10

# What If the Guiding Light Seems Dim?

Key: God's guidance is more like a lamp unto our feet than a lighthouse beaming far into the future.

*Life doesn't get much worse than having your brothers sell you into slavery. Unless you're Joseph. He'd accepted his fate, worked hard, and risen to top servant for an Egyptian, only to be thrown into jail for a crime he didn't commit.*

*In prison, Joseph again made the best of a bad situation and soon was put in charge of the prisoners. After he interpreted the dreams of two fellow captives, a cupbearer and a baker—people with direct access to Pharaoh, who could ask for a pardon—freedom must have seemed imminent. But the cupbearer forgot his promise to tell Pharaoh about Joseph.*

*Forgot, that is, for two years. Then Pharaoh started dreaming about harvests, cows, and scorched heads of grain. He gathered his magicians and wise men, but no one could interpret the dreams. Finally Pharaoh's cupbearer remembered the young man in the dungeon who had taken time to listen to dreams—and who knew what they meant.*

———

Joseph kept his eyes on the floor as he walked slowly toward the ruler of Egypt, his hands hidden in the folds of the borrowed robes so that no one could see them shaking. *Calm down,* he told himself. The ornate mosaics on which he stepped, though, emphasized the power and wealth of the man whose dreams he was to interpret. He tried to moisten his lips, but his tongue seemed made of sandpaper. What if he couldn't interpret Pharaoh's dream? Perhaps being hanged would be better than the dungeon . . .

*No,* he scolded himself, *think of other times you've listened to dreams . . . your own, the baker, the cupbearer.* Slowly, he managed to focus his thoughts on that afternoon in the dungeon two years before. The cupbearer had spoken in short, hurried sentences, as if to say, "I know you'll think this all nonsense . . ." His dream was a jumble of images: three vines, grapes, squeezing juice into Pharaoh's cup. Joseph knew what it meant before the man finished. The interpretation had bubbled from his lips, "Within three days Pharaoh will again make you his cupbearer."

*God told me,* Joseph reminded himself. His words to the cupbearer came from God, not from his own knowledge. But . . . was God interested in Pharaoh's dreams? *God, are you with me now?*

His eyes caught sight of the gilded platform of the throne. Quickly he bowed before Pharaoh, grateful for the clean tunic the guards had found for him. Whatever happened, he'd had this chance to bathe and walk about in the sunshine.

Then Pharaoh spoke. "I understand that when you hear of a dream, you can interpret it."

"It isn't me, but God who can give Pharaoh the answer he desires," Joseph heard his voice say as he glanced up quickly, then looked down again.

Pharaoh stared at him for a moment, then began, "In the dream, I stood on the bank of the Nile River. Seven fat cows, then seven emaciated ones, came out of the river. The scrawny animals devoured the fat ones, yet looked as ugly and lean as before.

"Then," Pharaoh went on, "I dreamed of seven beautiful heads of grain growing together. Seven others sprouted, only to be withered and scorched by the wind. The withered ones swallowed up the good grain. No one can explain these dreams to me."

*Plentiful harvest, then famine.* The interpretation filled Joseph's mind as he began to speak. He could feel his own voice grow stronger, more confident with God's wisdom as he shared how Egypt would need to store grain from the seven plentiful years. He concluded, "Let Pharaoh find a wise and discerning man to take charge of the harvests of Egypt so that food can be stored for the years of famine."

In the silence that followed those words, Joseph followed Pharaoh's gaze across the room to a table laden with grapes and breads, fish of every variety, quail and marrows, jars of honey and wine. *A famine? How?* his eyes seemed to say. Twisting the heavy ring that adorned his hand, Pharaoh stared in turn at each of the many officials who surrounded him.

*Now he'll sentence me to death,* Joseph thought. Still no one spoke.

Finally Pharaoh turned back to Joseph. "*You* are that man, and all my people are to submit to your orders. In you is the spirit of God."

*Am I dreaming now,* Joseph wondered as Pharaoh placed the signet ring on his finger. He, Joseph, a slave, a foreigner, was now second in command of all Egypt. It just couldn't be. Yet it was. It was all Joseph could do to keep from praising God out loud.

---

Just this once I wish God would tell me what to do. *We've all had that wish. A clear sign. A voice from heaven. A dream. However, did such clear guidance help Joseph see his future?*

*As a boy he dreamt that his brothers would all bow down to him, but even when Pharaoh put that ring on his finger, Joseph couldn't see how the dream would become reality when his brothers (the very same who had sold him into slavery) traveled to Egypt in search of food. Because of his position Joseph was able to provide for all of them and their extended families.*

*Yet at no point, despite dreams, did Joseph really understand what was coming next. Often that's how God's guidance works. We might get a vision of the future with no intermediate directions for how to get there. Or we may get a glimpse of the very next step in our journey, with no hint as to the final destination. The next stories tell of what it means to keep moving, one step at a time.*

Let the morning bring me word of your unfailing love,
for I have put my trust in you.
Show me the way I should go,
for to you I lift up my soul.[1]

## Nehemiah Who?

*By Karen J. Olson*

One January evening the only grandmother I had ever known passed away while I held her hand. In the days following I struggled to work through my grief. My sleep at night was sporadic at best, nonexistent at worst.

The evening before the funeral, I caught a whiff of the soap Grandma always used. That fragrance brought to mind her soft, cotton-white curls framing a face that held eighty-seven years' worth of gentle peaks, valleys, and well-worn trails. The image entwined with visions of her fingers crocheting intricate doilies, following patterns known in her heart. While the memories of the past mingled with the fresh, clean smell of the soap, I gradually dropped off into a restless, dream-laden slumber.

I dreamed of an old woman who crocheted bags made of sunlight and moonlight. The dream unfolded like a wondrous fairytale; a tale of the treasures within us and the journey we take to discover our gifts. I woke in the night with the title, *Much Needed Bags,* echoing in my head.

My family slept near me in the darkened room, so I couldn't get up to write the story. I knew with certainty, though, that I was supposed to. *I'll remember it in the morning,* I said to myself and sleep overcame me once more.

I dreamed the entire story again, rich in detail and color, with no deviation in script. This time when I woke up I wrote down the name *"Much Needed Bags"* on hotel stationery in the ethereal light of the midnight moon, so it wouldn't be forgotten in the reasonable light of the morning sun. I wanted to get up, go somewhere else and write the story immediately, but it just wasn't possible. At least, that's what I told myself.

Time passed. First days, then weeks, followed by months . . . then years. Each day as I sat down to write my other articles and columns, I felt a niggle in my stomach . . . I should be working on *Much Needed Bags*. But it was a children's book; I don't write children's stories. It was poetic in rhythm and cadence; I'm not a poet. Then I realized, *Karen, it's not about you. It's about all the times we chase after material prizes when the true riches we seek are inside us. We are so easily rerouted on our quest for the treasure buried within us.*

I looked at the blank Word document on my computer and typed,

"*Much Needed Bags* by Karen J. Olson." I paused, then began:

> Once there was an old woman with hair like a cloud that sat around her face like a warm summer mist. The face itself was wrinkled and wizened, but lit from within. A slight smile perpetually adorned it, just below her star-like eyes. She hummed a little tune as light as bird-song as she rocked,
> > rocked,
> > > rocked
>
> on her front porch in the sunny summer days, the chair creaking in cricket-time. She rocked near her fireplace in the windy winter, her shadow frolicking with the fire-flickered flames.

I stopped and sighed. I stared at the paragraph. I felt a knot form just below my breastbone. I took a deep breath and switched documents to work on an interview piece.

I shoved *Bags*, as I was now calling it, to the bottom of my "to do" pile again and finished my other assignments. The last piece of work in the pile, it stared up at me, waiting patiently. I opened the document and flexed my fingers. I waited five minutes, then I shut down my computer and left the room . . . again.

For the first time in my life I was afraid to write something.

I busied myself with my columns and features. Each time I felt unrest about the project, I pushed it back, telling myself I'd get to it. *God understands that I have other things to do,* I thought. *It's not like I'm disobeying, really; I'm just waiting for the right time.*

Two years after my grandmother's death, on a subzero blizzardy night in January, I got ready for bed. I shivered as I jumped in, clad in a pair of men's blue-and-green plaid flannel pajama bottoms, mottled gray and neon orange wool hunting socks and a long-sleeved Henley T-shirt in an eye-zapping shade of turquoise. I snuggled into my bed, exhausted from working all day and shoveling the mountains of drift-packed snow. As usual, it took me a while to create a nest comfortable enough to fall asleep in. Once asleep, however, I slept hard.

I woke up suddenly at a sound in the dark. I looked at the alarm clock—2:12 A.M. I listened intently but heard nothing. I lay back down and started to drift off. Then I heard it again:

"Nehemiah," the voice said audibly.

I sat up, clutched the quilt to my chest, and blinked hard to clear my eyes, trying to see where the sound came from.

"What?!" I whispered into the dark, "What?!"

"Nehemiah," I heard again.

I sat in stunned silence, then lurched for the pen on the bedside table and, with a shaking hand, wrote "Nehemiah" on my note pad. I set the pad back on the table and listened for a few seconds. I pinched my arm—hard—to see if I was dreaming. I wasn't. Holding my breath, I strained to hear. Then, abruptly overcome by fatigue, I leaned back and fell asleep.

The next day I began my morning routine and saw the note on my bedside table.

*Nehemiah.*

I felt a trickle of fear . . . Nehemiah? What was it all about? Was Nehemiah a book in the Bible? With a sense of dread I dragged myself to the living room and checked my Bible. There it was . . . *Nehemiah.* I sighed in relief. Still, I set the Bible down and delayed reading further.

I made a cup of coffee and some toast. I put in a load of wash. I took the dog out and stood there, thinking how I should be showing the same devotion to the Lord that my dog showed me—running eagerly to obey me, full of joyous expectation.

Finally, after I ran out of other things to do, I picked up the Bible and began reading the story of Nehemiah. When I finished I wondered why I'd been afraid. I felt light and airy, happy and loved.

Nehemiah was instructed to build the walls of Jerusalem, but the city was still being attacked by raiding parties. To get the job done he allocated his resources. Some men continued to build the wall exclusively, other men protected the city from raiders, making sure that the walls were safe while Nehemiah worked on rebuilding the damaged areas.

A third group did both. They helped build the walls with a brick in one hand and helped protect the city with a sword in the other. *The story is the wall I want you to build, Karen.* It was fine to work on other articles and projects to protect my income, but I needed to allocate some of my resources toward writing the story of *Much Needed Bags.*

The relief I felt was like that of a child when her parent comes in to help her deal with a messy room. I had put off writing the story for so long that I felt hopelessly lost trying to fit it into my life. God's loving hand gently guided me back on the path with love and kindness. There was no anger, just an overwhelming sense of being cherished. *"I'm right here, Karen. I love you and I won't abandon you."*

Now I work on the story every Friday. Some weeks I write three pages, other weeks I write a sentence or two, but I am building the walls brick by brick. I've told my friends the story and they tease me about the book; they smile and joke about my tangle with *Bags*. They understand about getting lost.

More importantly, so does God.

---

*Karen J. Olson is a writer and columnist who lives in Wisconsin. A few months after writing this story, she finished the rough draft of* Much Needed Bags. *Now whenever she's feeling overwhelmed, overworked, and underappreciated, she turns to work on the revisions for* Bags. *She relaxes in her recliner with a cup of tea and her editing pen. Snuggled in her favorite rose-peppered blanket, she is reminded of the incredible depth of God's love and faithfulness.*

## A Quiet Promise
*By Jane McClain*

As I entered the church lounge I snapped on just one row of lights. For our early Saturday prayer meeting, semidarkness worked best. Before taking my usual place on the floor where I could rest my back against one of the comfy sofas, I pulled over a couple of folding chairs to add to the lopsided circle of couches and stuffed chairs. I never knew how many people would come.

The sweater I'd tossed on felt good on this crisp fall morning. My Bible on the floor in front of me, I paged through the Psalms, then looked at my watch. Already 7:10 and I was the only one. *Lord, keep everyone safe as they travel here today.* My mind wandered over the names of people we'd be praying for, concerns of the church. Seven-fifteen and still no one else had come. This wasn't normal. Usually people arrived saying, "God woke me up at six o'clock this morning, so I thought I'd better come."

I listened but didn't hear any footsteps coming down the hall. I checked the side door. Yes, it was unlocked. *God,* I wondered, *am I the only one who missed your message to sleep in this morning? Or is this prayer meeting not all that important?* No, that wasn't true. I'd felt God's presence so many times as we'd gathered for prayer and joyous song. Numbers didn't matter; Jesus was present when even two gathered in His name. And there'd always been more than two, except this morning.

Surely God wanted prayer. Was I somehow failing to lead this group properly? Still alone, I bowed my head, then lay on the carpet with my arms stretched out in front of me, and prayed aloud, "Lord, I believe you want us to pray. I believe you have many people in our church whom you are calling to prayer. Raise up those people to become the pray-ers you want them to be."

The door opened. Startled, I looked up. A staff member, not one of my Saturday group, entered. "Are you all right?" he asked. I nodded and explained what I was doing. He still looked puzzled. I prayed for a while longer, then headed home.

The next week, two or three people joined me. As fall turned to winter, I could count on Viv and Jim, two young adults who attended faithfully, with a few occasional drop-ins. We prayed fervently, but also laughed together and ministered to each other. *"Whenever two or more are gathered . . ."* I kept telling myself.

One day as I sorted my laundry in the basement, a thought passed quietly through my head: *"Sunday . . . more ministry. Meet on Sundays, not Saturdays."* The thought came unbidden. Was that the Lord? I didn't know. And what could "more ministry" mean? More people? Praying directly for the worship team? Praying for requests made during the service? Nothing seemed obvious, so I let the message slide. After all, it might just have been a passing thought.

But over the next several weeks the quiet thought returned more than once. As I walked along the tree-lined streets of my neighborhood, I asked, "Lord, what does 'more ministry' mean?" New ideas flooded my mind. If I didn't have a Saturday prayer group, my husband and I would have more choices of when to visit his parents who lived a hundred miles west of us. That could mean more ministry to them. Would I be able to spend more time with my own dad, who had Alzheimer's? Would more people come on Sunday? Would more people's lives be changed? I had no clue if the actual Sunday group would produce more fruit than the Saturday group. It was a risk.

I brought the idea up to my husband at supper, with a catch. "If I move the meeting to Sunday, I'll have to pray during the eight-thirty service and attend with you at eleven. We'll have to drive separately."

"That's okay. We can do that," he responded. That excuse was taken away. The quiet whisper, *"Sunday . . . more ministry,"* grew stronger.

One Saturday I told my two faithful pray-ers, "I'm thinking of changing our group to Sunday morning. I feel God is telling me to do this to have more ministry, although I don't know what ministry God means."

"I can't come on Sunday," Jim said. "I bring my neighbor boy to Sunday school and I need to keep doing that."

"I can't either," Viv apologized. "I do so much with my kids and grandkids on Sundays and I need to keep that time open."

Could changing to Sundays be the right thing if Jim and Viv couldn't come? Still, the phrase, *"Sunday . . . more ministry,"* kept returning. I needed to listen. I called several people who had joined us occasionally. When one agreed to join me on Sundays, I put my ad in the bulletin.

"Join with others to pray for our church during the first service. 8:30 A.M. Room 326."

Within a few weeks, two people grew to five, then to eight—committed people who set their alarms to come. One woman has been with me almost the whole eleven years we've been meeting. Two others are also long-term members. Others come and go. We've seen answers to small prayers and large ones. A cancer healed, a child adopted, our church going from renting a school to having our own building.

Meeting in our own room during a service has allowed us to be connected in ways I couldn't have thought of. As we hear worship songs being sung, we pray for the power of God's presence to be real to people. When the congregation quiets for the sermon, we know to pray for their hearts to be touched with God's message for their lives.

We also meet with the staff and worship team before the service, discussing the theme for the day so that we can pray more effectively for our ministers and the congregation.

And out of these prayers has sprung another, much larger group that receives monthly e-mails of how to pray for our church and weekly updates on what to pray for the weekend services. Why Sundays instead of Saturdays? I don't know. Perhaps our connections with staff and the service increased others' awareness of the need for prayer. I still lead a very small group, yet its influence has spread. More people are praying, not because of my leadership but because that quiet promise of *"more ministry"* wouldn't go away until I listened.

————

*Jane is always glad when the Lord speaks to her and she under-stands. Sometimes it is a matter of calling someone that she's been think-ing about and finding that the timing of the call is perfect and blesses her friend. Once it was to take a certain turn in a walk around the neighbor-hood, which led her to an acquaintance who had experienced a trauma the night before. Jane could then listen to her and pray for her.*

## Was I at Fault?
*By Jane Kise*

Kelly's[2] words hit me like a hard punch to the stomach. "Of course I haven't returned your phone calls—I was too angry. Not only did you over-bill me for the last project, but your error in the presentation materials made me look like a fool."

My thoughts crashed into each other. Overbill her? Me, who never even made personal copies at work without paying for them? I'd called her about the expense portion, asking her to pay only what she thought was proper. Had she forgotten? Didn't she trust my integrity?

The two of us had worked together on various consulting efforts for several years. We'd *never* had a disagreement. I wanted to snap, "Don't you remember our conversations?" but something held my tongue. Instead, I said, "You've really caught me off guard with this and I need to think through what you've said. Would you have time to talk tomorrow?"

"I'll call at two. By then I'll have made up my mind," she said as our conversation ended.

I sat back in my chair, stunned. Making up her mind meant that my livelihood, my reputation in our industry, and the several thousand dollars she owed me were at stake. For me, consulting meant more time at home with my two preschoolers and the freedom to match their schedules. Kelly, though, had the credentials, found the clients. Without her, I couldn't do the work.

My face grew hot as I remembered the error she'd just thrown back in my face. We'd met the night before a client's board meeting, at 9:30. When I arrived at her house she hadn't quite finished tucking her children in for the night. Finally at 9:50, she sunk wearily into a chair at the dining room table, where I'd been waiting. "I have to chaperone a field trip tomorrow, of all things," she told me. "You can handle getting the notebooks together, right?"

She was in charge, so I said, "Of course."

Because it was so late, she simply handed me all of her notes. We never discussed the presentation or the issues. Her part of the project wasn't even compiled into spreadsheets yet. The next day seemed to fast-forward as I reviewed her data as well as mine, created the graphs and reports, and sped to the copy shop. By the time I stepped into the shower, I really should have been stepping on the gas to get to the meeting. I was more surprised that I'd only made *one* error in those lengthy notebooks. And the typo was only a report date!

I felt physically sick over the whole situation. I seldom kneel to pray, but that afternoon I shoved back my chair, closed up my work files, and got down on my knees.

How could I show Kelly that she'd misjudged me? *God, you have to help me listen to Kelly tomorrow without being defensive—and without giving way to tears. I have no idea what to say to her that won't sound like whining. She's got this so wrong. . . .*

*"Jane,"* an answer came almost immediately, *"What you* did *doesn't matter; it's what she* saw *that counts."*

*God, my honesty doesn't matter? She's the one who didn't listen. Or warn me that the reports were mine to write and produce. Why should I . . .* My angry thoughts trailed off even as they formed. What *had* Kelly seen? The accusations were so off . . . was something else happening to Kelly? Was she worried about one of her daughters? Finances? Health concerns? What could have fueled such anger?

Slowly, thoroughly, I reviewed our years together. While I can honestly say I wasn't guilty of the things Kelly accused me of, there were things I'd both done and not done that had fueled Kelly's conclusions.

I *hadn't* been honest about how tight deadlines affected me. While her performance seemed to improve under pressure, I fell apart—hence the report mistake.

I *hadn't* been honest about the role I hoped to play. As I thought over the last months, I realized that Kelly was pushing me toward the details of the business—working with client finances, overseeing regulatory requirements, etc. Those were the areas where she most needed help. Unfortunately, I couldn't handle details any better than she did. We both thrived on client contact and helping them solidify their missions and envision new directions.

The partnership had seemed so ideal. I thought we'd been more than colleagues, sharing maternity clothes, running together, and confiding in each other about dreams and doubts. Plus, the work fit my family's needs. My toddlers were only in day care twelve hours a week, and the pay made my work hours worthwhile. I *liked* the prestige of being a consultant. And I knew I couldn't continue on my own without her credentials.

*God, my guess is it's over, my fault or not,* I concluded. Tears filled my eyes at that thought. What would I do? I pushed panic aside and instead prayed for how to restore her trust in me, that our friendship might continue even if our partnership was over.

As I steeled myself for her phone call the next day, two things seemed absent from my thoughts: I dropped the idea of explaining my actions, and something held me back from brainstorming how to save the partnership, in spite of the frightening truth that I had no other good career options. *"Concentrate on Kelly,"* God seemed to be saying.

The phone call was brief; we agreed to meet in person at a local pancake house. As I slid into the booth across from Kelly, her smile held warmth, not anger. She began, "Now that I've had a chance to cool off, I need to apologize for overreacting. Let's let all that go and . . . I think the bigger issue for me is that I'm better working alone, not with a partner."

"That actually makes sense," I said, masking fairly well, I think, the sense of loss I felt at her words. But it *did* make sense, with her last-minute nature and intuitive way of running the business.

Kelly explained her plans and then said, "I want to be fair to you; this is my change of plans, not yours. So why don't you take those two out-state jobs we already contracted. That should tide you over while you build your own business."

I stared at the client folders she handed over. The funds would pay my day care expenses for the next twelve months, giving me true freedom to explore new options for work and my family. I had no idea what I'd do, but Kelly was giving me time to decide.

Kelly said more than once, "I never thought we'd be able to discuss this rationally." We parted with mutual respect, my overwhelming desire ever since her anger had sent me to my knees. I had no idea where I was headed, but with two clients in hand, and the memory of how God had helped me navigate the misunderstandings with Kelly, I figured I could take on the future, one step at a time.

---

*That meeting marked the start of a slow, slow journey toward my own writing and consulting business in an entirely different field. My husband and I both liked having me home with the children. He agreed that those initial clients gave me a cushion for exploring becoming a published author—not exactly a path to steady employment, but something we'd talked about for years.*

*As I finished those jobs, a neighbor called with an emergency consulting need for her firm. My receipts from that paid most of the next year's part-time day care bills. The next year she had a similar need. Still, those weren't writing jobs. I joined a church task force to develop curriculum, knowing I'd have to write there.*

*The next year I was hired by another member of the task force, Sandra Hirsh, to edit a book. She asked me to coauthor a second one. Our curriculum became our book, LifeKeys.*

*Before I knew it, I'd coauthored two books and had joined Sandra in team building and coaching, a far cry from my financial work with Kelly. At no step along the way, though, did I understand where I was headed.*

*I still counsel aspiring writers, "Don't quit your day job." However, when I lost mine, God helped me keep walking, one step at a time, into a future that fits how I was created.*

## KEY: God's guidance is more like a lamp unto our feet than a lighthouse beaming far into the future.

A little at a time—that's frequently how God guides us. When the Bible describes a lamp illuminating our path, we somehow think we should be able to see farther ahead than one or two steps. However, what does it really mean to be guided by a lamp?

For one thing, it's dark out. It's hard to see where you're going.

Remember, too, that lamps in biblical times were uneven wicks suspended in little vessels of oil. They provided flickering, smoky illumination, not the steady beam of a searchlight or even a flashlight.

And even with a strong flashlight in the darkness, it's safer to take one step at a time, not run ahead quickly. The light doesn't take away the darkness; it simply allows you to keep walking in the blackest of nights.

When you think it's too dark to keep moving—perhaps the darkness comes from doubts or the difficulty of uncertainty—remember how little the Israelites benefited from being guided constantly through the wilderness, by a pillar of clouds during the day and one of fire by night. That certainty bred disbelief and unrest, not faith and trust.

If the messages from signs and circumstances don't give enough light, remember how you were created and seek out wisdom from the Bible. Concentrate on lighting your way from all of these sources. You won't end up far from where God wants you to be.

> *It's dark, Lord.*
> *Shadows creep about me, my fears of*
> *failing,*
> > *straying,*
> > > *falling,*
> > *halt my footsteps, hinder my way.*
> *Yet even here in the shadows,*
> *the sparks of your love flicker, then glow,*
> *pointing to my next step . . .*
> *when I accept that You are all I need to press on. Amen.*

---

[1]Psalm 143:8
[2]Names and certain details have been changed.

# 11

# How Can I Plan If My Future Is in God's Hands?

**Key: Living within God's will means looking for God, listening for God, talking with God, all without ceasing.**

*As heart-wrenching as infertility is today, it was a horrific fate for women in biblical times. Children were their status symbols. Barrenness left a woman vulnerable to ridicule. Further, they were ignorant of medical causes and believed that infertility always and only stemmed from being out of God's favor.*

*The first chapter of 1 Samuel tells the story of Hannah. Her husband had two wives. Hannah's rival Peninnah bore several children. Peninnah made Hannah's life miserable, goading her to tears because she couldn't conceive.*

*What kind of future lay in store for Hannah? Shame and teasing only emphasizing the empty arms that longed to hold a child of her own? So Hannah made a seemingly rash vow: Remember me, O Lord Almighty, give me a son, and I will give him to the Lord for all the days of his life.*

―――――

Hannah tugged at the stitches she'd just sewn, then broke off the thread. Samuel's new robe was completed. She'd left a bit of extra fabric tucked into the hemline in case she'd guessed wrong as to how much he'd grown in the last twelve months.

Five years old now. She'd see him tomorrow. Tomorrow they'd make the daylong journey to Shiloh for the annual sacrifice.

Shiloh. The house of the Lord. The true home of her heart because Samuel lived there. In that place six years ago, she'd made her vow. There, two years ago, she'd left the son God gave her in the care of the old priest Eli. Three years old, his wavy, uncut hair curling below his ears, grasping her finger even as his eyes, full of curiosity, explored his new home. His permanent home.

*But he remembered me,* she consoled herself. She smiled at the memory of four-year-old Samuel a year ago on the day of their sacrifice, standing obediently next to Eli as they approached, although the way he rose on tiptoes over and over revealed his excitement at seeing his parents. To only see him once a year . . . it really was enough!

Peninnah had shaken her head in disbelief when Hannah explained her vow all those years ago, saying, "You waited all this time for a son, for nothing? You'll be childless for a second time."

"No, I have a son. That will not change. But he belongs to God, not me," she'd said firmly. *And I will never let myself regret my vow,* she added to herself.

And she hadn't. Three years of memories continually renewed her thankfulness. Samuel's first smile, first step, first tug at her robe to get her attention—she'd stored each image in preparation for the years to follow, determined to draw on them as gifts from God. Slowly she smoothed out each wrinkle in Samuel's new robe, then folded it to fit into her bundle for the journey. But before she tucked it away, she pressed the robe against her chest, hugging it long and hard. *There, hugs to last another year. . . .*

———

*Some might argue that Hannah bargained with God to get the son she yearned for. Yet she asked for and relinquished a child in one breath.*

*Hannah didn't know whether her husband would honor her vow—he had the right to overturn it. Or that Eli would do a good job in raising Samuel—his own sons are called wicked. Or that her future held five more children—until long after she'd given Samuel back to God. She simply made her vow and left her future in God's hands.*

*That's the level of trust we need when we seek God's guidance. Like the people in the next stories, we need to be able to say, "I trust you, Lord. Even though I don't understand why you're leading me in this direction, I'm still coming with you."*

Trust in the Lord with all your heart and lean not on your own understanding; in all your ways acknowledge him, and he will make your paths straight.[1]

## I Will Never . . .
### By Noel Piper

"I will never marry a preacher! A doctor would be okay, but a preacher? Never!" I can point to the very spot in the freshman dorm where I stood that day in 1966 mapping out my future. It never occurred to me that any preacher hearing my pronouncement would have sighed in relief.

I didn't know much about being a pastor's wife, but I was pretty sure it wouldn't leave room for the impromptu fun I loved—like dancing with friends in the campus fountain one particularly hot June night. A college trustee happened past as we splashed and hooted. He aimed a shaking finger at us and demanded, "Who do you think are you? A bunch of existentialists?"

*Existentialist?* I wondered silently. *What's that? Somebody who is glad to exist?*

That same month, I met a cute guy with soft brown curls brushing his collar. Johnny was a fun-loving literature major, also pre-med. I was glad *he* existed. *And* he liked me. Perfect! It didn't take many ice cream cones, bags of popcorn, and hours of singing along with the Beach Boys before we were talking about marriage.

At the beginning of the next semester, mononucleosis confined Johnny to bed in the college infirmary. Each morning on the campus radio station, he heard Dr. Harold Ockenga's chapel service sermon. Each afternoon I heard, "Oh, I'd love to be able to handle the Scriptures like that!"

For two weeks Johnny lay there stewing, "I'll never catch up in Organic Chemistry, but I have to have it to continue in the pre-med program. I wonder . . ." Dr. Ockenga's sermons had stirred his soul. He dropped the idea of med school and set his sights on seminary instead. I hadn't told him what I thought about marrying a preacher, but by now I was way more interested in *him* than in his future profession. Anyway, he thought he'd probably become a biblically grounded English teacher, so I was safe. We were married just after he began seminary.

Together we dived right into the routines of real life. "Reality" for me meant hundreds of hours at our rickety gray metal typing table, typing Johnny's papers. He did all the serious study while I soaked up the results as my fingers flew across the keys. Not fun, but interesting. Intriguing, even.

"Looks like we'll be going overseas," my husband said as he read the rejection from the American university where he'd applied to pursue his doctoral degree. Once we moved to Germany, there were *more* papers to type and retype, including hundreds of dissertation pages. Making a fool of myself trying to speak German was not fun, but it was useful for the daily trek to the market and for learning from the other tenants about my responsibility to take a turn cleaning the apartment stairway. It was fun visiting castles and museums, and our eyes were opened to see the world through the window of another culture. Christmas, for example, seemed much simpler and closer to a real celebration of the Christ.

A phone call from home broke into our new routine and taught us that reality is sometimes difficult to bear. My sixteen-year-old brother Ben had died at a country-road intersection in Georgia, too far away for me to join my family. So we cried alone in Munich. But not alone, because the very next Sunday at church we met Al and Virginia, who took us under their wings and became the kind of friends who last a lifetime.

Less than a year later they laughed along with us as we thanked God for our first child. The joy I felt then was deeper than any fun I'd ever experienced, better by far than fountain dancing. Yet the day we brought new-born Karsten home from the hospital, I stood in our living room and thought, "Two of us walked out the door at four A.M. the other day, and now we are three until one of us dies. Speaking of which, how *do* you keep a baby alive? I can't even keep my rubber plant from a slow death!" As I realized our total dependence on God, fun was not on my mind.

Karsten certainly brought moments of great fun into our lives. I could hardly imagine what our chubby blond baby would be when he grew up. Fun, though, had slipped way down on my must-have list. What I wanted most deeply was that Karsten be God's forever, and I knew I couldn't make that happen. *Lord, I need your wisdom,* I prayed, turning to God's promise, "If any of you is lacking in wisdom, ask God, who gives to all generously and ungrudgingly, and it will be given you."[2]

Just after Karsten's first birthday a Christian college offered Johnny the kind of position we had been praying for, teaching New Testament. First-time courses meant late nights of preparation for him and early mornings of typing for me. That was not fun for a night person, but what did that matter? We could hardly believe God had provided a situation where someone was willing to pay John to do what he loved.

We found a lively church where the preaching of God's word shaped and focused our faith. As our family grew, our lives revolved around our church. John taught an adult Sunday school class while I became involved in various ministries. Most of our best friends were part of that body, the ones we prayed with and leaned on in hard times as well as the ones who joined us for spur-of-the-moment fun.

When our pastor moved to another ministry, the church went through several months of visitors in the pulpit. Riding home in our boxy little Fiat station wagon, I knew what to expect. After a good sermon, Johnny sighed wistfully, "Oh, I'd like to do that." After a not-so-good sermon, he banged his fist on the steering wheel, "Somebody's got to do better than that!"

One morning in the season when we were awaiting our third child, my husband leaned toward me as dawn broke and whispered, "Are you awake?"

"I am now," I mumbled into my pillow.

"What would you say if I told you I wanted to become a pastor?" he asked.

I didn't have to wake up fully to answer instantly and wholeheartedly, "I've seen it coming for a long time. I'll be happy with whatever God leads you to do."

All the time, I had thought I was praying for wisdom simply to be a better mother for my children's sake. God, as usual, gave far more than I asked. From the day that fun-seeking girl had made her sophomoric freshman pronouncement until the morning of my husband's life-changing question, fourteen years had passed. God had spent those years changing my heart, patiently making me a woman who still enjoyed fun but knew surely that faith, hope, and love were far greater. God's wisdom reshaped my will so that I could rejoice when my husband discerned his true calling as a preacher. Thanks to God, I was now married to a preacher after all!

*After being married to a student for six years and a professor for six years, Noel became a pastor's wife in 1980. She thanks God that they are all the same man. She and John have five children and a growing number of grandchildren. They provide reason for Noel to keep praying for wisdom, especially when she remembers her own youthful silliness. In college, for instance, when Noel thought she had life planned, she avoided classes requiring writing because she didn't like to write. Now she is the author of* Treasuring God in Our Traditions *and* Most of All, Jesus Loves You.

## Counting the Cost

*Paul Tschida*
*As told to Sharon Sheppard*

"You were almost a widow tonight," I whispered to my wife, Lila, when I slipped into our bedroom around five o'clock one morning.

"I know," she responded groggily.

"You *do*? Did the hospital call you?"

"No, God woke me at 1:28 and told me to pray for you."

I was stunned. I'd had shotgun pellets whizzing past me at exactly 1:28 that morning. I couldn't shrug off my wife's prayer as a coincidence. As a rural deputy sheriff in Morrison County, Minnesota, I normally didn't see much criminal action.

I'd received a call from a frantic young man who said his drunken brother was threatening the family with a gun. I radioed for reinforcements. As we converged on the scene a raw December wind whistled across the prairie. Bare branches scraped against the frost-covered windows.

My partner and I circled the house, looking for a window clear enough to see through. Finding a partially clear pane, we peered in at the scene. Yelling and threatening, the brother was wrestling with the deranged man outside the door of the room where his mother and teenaged brother cowered in fear.

Before we could gain access to the house, the gunman spotted us, shoved his brother aside, and started firing. Pellets streaked between my partner and me, grazing the deputy's leg and riddling my jacket with holes, but never touching my flesh. We ran around to the front of the house, broke down the door, and wrestled the man to the floor.

I pondered my wife's urgent call to prayer for my safety at the exact time I was in danger. Could prayer be *that* important? Oh, I believed in it, but I'd been raised in a church that didn't emphasize personal prayer. I figured God was telling me to change.

From that day on, I began to pray more and more. At first, I asked for guidance as I drove to each emergency call instead of just running through all of the possible scenarios. But then, not long after the shootout incident, I had to inform a woman that her husband had been killed. Tears streaked down her cheeks as she tried to keep from sobbing out loud. I murmured, "Would you like me to pray?"

"Oh yes," she managed to say, so I took her by the hand and prayed, "Lord, please comfort her and grant her peace. Calm her heart and hold her in your arms." Since then she has thanked me for that prayer again and again. *God,* I thought, *you're telling me that prayer is fully part of my job, aren't you?*

I didn't set out intentionally to pray aloud at work, in my sheriff's uniform, but asking God for help when people really needed it seemed the only right thing to do. I knew about separation of church and state, but people's needs knew no such boundaries. Somehow my co-workers started seeking me out. "Paul, would you pray for me?" or "My daughter is going through a rough time right now. . . ."

Then tragedy struck home. Just a week after the September 11 terrorist attacks, as our seventeen-year-old son, Mark, drove to school one morning, a gravel truck came barreling through an intersection and plowed into him, killing him instantly.

In the midst of our grief, I had to decide whether to run for reelection for a sixth term as county sheriff. In the past, I'd won quite easily, even running unopposed a few times. This time, however, one of my deputies was running against me. There were rumblings about my mixing religion with work, praying on the job. Did I have the will or the energy to campaign? Did I really want the job again? After prayer, Lila and I still felt uncertain. "God, show us your will," we prayed.

One weekend, exhausted and grieving, Lila and I went up to our lake cabin to rest and think. We attended Sunday service at a nearby church. A guest speaker preached from Hebrews 12, "Let us run with perseverance the race marked out for us," he read. "Let us fix our eyes on

Jesus. . . . Consider him who endured such opposition from sinful men, so that you will not grow weary and lose heart. . . . Therefore, strengthen your feeble arms and weak knees."[3]

We jumped back into the race. My opponent waged an aggressive campaign, and I lost.

"Weren't you devastated by losing the election?" people sometimes ask.

"When you've lost a son," I say, "losing an election is nothing."

Still at first I wondered why God had seemingly asked me to run, knowing that I'd lose. Lila and I pondered that question and realized that all the activity had given us something to focus on besides the loss of our son. As we went door-to-door throughout the county, virtually everyone asked, "How are you doing?" Whether or not they intended to vote for me, they expressed genuine concern over Mark's death. Wonderful conversations evolved as we shared how God was helping us cope. And we were amazed to discover how many other families in the community had also lost children.

I don't know if my praying on the job cost me the election, but what happened next convinced me that I'd been doing exactly what God wanted me to do. I received seven job offers and finally settled on being chief deputy of Carver County. My staff and budget are much larger, and I see a lot more action. Even better, as a deputy I don't have to keep running for reelection.

The late-night call from God to my wife that December night wasn't just about my safety. It was my own wake-up call to revitalize my prayer life in preparation for changes God had in store for me.

———

*One of the most gratifying things about freelancing, Sharon says, is the opportunity to meet ordinary people who've done extraordinary things. She first heard this story from Paul's wife, Lila, when they were in a Bible study group together. Later, when she met Paul, she was deeply moved by his commitment. "His willingness to put his job on the line for his faith earned my abiding respect," says Sharon. "He'd get my vote any day!"*

## Setting My Plans Aside
*By Linda Gilligan*

When I was five years old, my mother and I went to a neighbor's house for coffee. I loved to drink coffee like the grown-ups. My cup contained milk with just enough coffee to give it a little color.

I also loved listening to grown-up conversations, interesting and yet mysterious. This morning, my mother and Bev were talking about someone's wedding. I'd already planned my wedding, so I joined their conversation by announcing, "I'm getting married when I'm twenty-five years old."

Mom and Bev had a good laugh about that! But that is exactly what I did. I married my college sweetheart, Tom, a few months before my twenty-sixth birthday.

Setting long-term goals for myself and planning how to achieve them, that was me. Before I left elementary school, I'd planned out my education, career, and family. College definitely, then a good job that allowed me to support myself, and finally marriage and several children.

Year by year, I checked off one goal after another. By the time I was a young adult, my successes in the world of finance gave me the sense that I was in control of my life. With a good plan, I could accomplish anything.

And children and family were top priorities. Tom and I both came from large families—I was the oldest of five and he was the oldest of ten. We planned to have our first child just a few years after we married.

In the meantime, we looked for ways to be with children. Tom helped coach my brother's baseball team. I taught religious education at my church. Together we mentored youth at a school for the visually impaired. "You'll make such great parents," was a comment we heard over and over.

My plan included having children before my thirtieth birthday. Everything I read in the popular press said that it was best for women to have children by then. But I passed that milestone without becoming pregnant. Friends, sisters, and sisters-in-law were having babies all around me. When would it be my turn? I felt I needed to take control of things and get my plans back on track.

We sought help from fertility specialists. Three years dragged by with increasingly complicated tests and procedures, but none of the experts could explain why I couldn't get pregnant. Each new test or procedure renewed our hope of either having a child or finding answers. Our hope turned to grief with every menstrual cycle and inconclusive test.

After months of this emotional roller coaster, my dreams turned to despair. *You're a failure, you have no plans without children.* We had just built a new home; our footsteps echoed through rooms designed for cribs and bunk beds. In spite of a major promotion at work, I felt as if everything I'd worked toward was slipping through my fingers. I'd lost control.

One crisp morning when I left my house for work, sorrow slowed my steps and sent tears to my eyes. As I crossed the street toward the bus stop, I pulled my jacket tighter around me and prayed, "Holy Spirit, please help me!" Suddenly my entire being was filled with the greatest peace I have ever experienced. I stopped and took a deep breath. What just happened? The despair and desperation were gone. God seemed to say to me, *"Linda, I am with you. You will find your purpose in life. Everything will be all right."*

Once again I could think clearly, yet I had to ponder God's message for a few weeks before I understood the bigger implication: Maybe God's plan for our future was *different* than mine. I would have to keep my heart open to listen and learn what it was, praying for guidance on leading a fulfilling life *without* children.

Tom agreed to take a break from actively pursuing pregnancy. Without the repetitive hope-turned-to-grieving cycle, I began living again. Whether or not we had children, our lives were filled with blessings. And since the choice seemed out of our hands, we'd be thankful for freedom to do things that parents could not.

We took some time for ourselves. We played lots of racquetball, took long runs, and enjoyed attending plays and musicals. We bought a fishing boat, delighting in fishing adventures on northern Minnesota lakes. We took several trips each summer, but one of our favorite times to fish was mid-September after all the children were back in school. Then we had the entire lake to ourselves. I decided to pursue a difficult financial certification program, expanding my professional knowledge, since my career and not motherhood was to be my main activity.

We also embraced the extra time we had for others. I headed the worship board at my church and learned much about the richness of liturgy. Tom and I still interacted with young people on a regular basis through our family, friends, and neighbors. Life was very full and very rewarding; I felt I was making a positive contribution to those around me.

After taking a break for more than a year, Tom and I decided to go through with a diagnostic test that I had never completed. We'd make one last effort to become parents before giving it up for good. I'd have closure, knowing that I'd done everything I could reasonably do in my pursuit of motherhood. Then I planned to move on with my life and not look back.

I never had the test. When I went in for a doctor's appointment a few days before the procedure was scheduled, I felt almost sheepish as I said, "This may sound crazy, but I'm thinking I might actually be pregnant."

A slight lift of his eyebrows betrayed his skepticism, but he said, "Then we'd better order a different test today."

I was indeed pregnant! Maybe God wanted me to be a mom after all!

Emily was born after a somewhat difficult pregnancy and delivery. She was a special baby, since we had waited so long! I *knew* that this would be my only child, so we were going to celebrate every holiday and birthday in an extreme manner. I would make all her Halloween costumes, even though I hated to sew. I would bake all her cakes from scratch. I would read to her every night. Now that I finally had the chance, I was going to be the best parent that I could!

Talk about not guessing God's plan for me—Emily is not my only child. Two years later, daughter Molly was born. One year after that, James was born. Nine years later, just before my forty-eighth birthday, Margaret was born.

Today I smile and shake my head when I think about all the plans I made for parenting. We *do* celebrate all holidays and birthdays (the children won't let me stop celebrating mine!), but I haven't had time to sew anything for years. I have baked some cakes from scratch, although they have been few and far between. The last birthday cake I made was more than two years ago when Molly wanted a three-layer chocolate cake. It was a bit lopsided but tasted fine. We do try to read most nights. But now I know that parenting is a job that will never be perfected or finished.

Tom reminds me to live for today and not get too carried away with planning the future. My children have taught me that you can only plan things up to a certain point. I still like to set goals, plan, and think long term, but I've learned that God's plans can be more wonderful than the ones I devise!

————

*Linda believes that accepting Maggie's surprise arrival as she turned forty-eight would have been much harder if she hadn't learned earlier to wait and see what God had in mind! The older children are doting baby-sitters and also provide constant entertainment as Maggie watches and cheers at their soccer and hockey games.*

## KEY: Living within God's will means looking for God, listening for God, talking with God, all without ceasing.

So much of our future lies outside our control, even when we think we're following God's lead. We're dependent on the decisions of others, our health, the events around us, the whims of those we work for. "Why plan?" you might say, a sentiment echoed in the writings of James:

> Now listen, you who say, "Today or tomorrow we will go to this or that city, spend a year there, carry on business and make money." Why, you do not even know what will happen tomorrow . . . Instead, you ought to say, "If it is the Lord's will, we will live and do this or that." As it is, you boast and brag.[4]

Yet all of us have plans, or hopes or dreams. Other verses in Proverbs assure us that planning can be godly.

> But those who plan what is good find love and faithfulness.[5]
> The plans of the diligent lead to profit as surely as haste leads to poverty.[6]
> Commit to the Lord whatever you do, and your plans will succeed.[7]

The truth is, whether we plan or not, we can't be sure of where we're going. Our futures are in God's hands. God will be with us, whether that future includes children or not, the job we wanted or not, the ideal marriage, or whatever our own plans include. So as we plan we need to hold lightly to those hopes and dreams. Understand what we can and cannot change. Believe that God loves us, no matter what life throws our way. And keep listening for God, praying without ceasing.

*Lord, my plans . . .*
*   here they are . . .*
*      are they yours?*
*I may not have it right*
*   yet life is racing on.*
*   I can't sit still. So*
*I'll keep listening for you, each step into the future,*
*   for no matter where I go, you will be with me. Amen.*

---

[1] Proverbs 3:5–6
[2] James 1:5 NRSV
[3] Hebrews 12:1–3, 12
[4] James 4:13–16
[5] Proverbs 14:22
[6] Proverbs 21:5
[7] Proverbs 16:3

# 12

# What If I Missed God's Plan?

**Key: No matter how or why you stumble, God stands ready to show you how to return to what you were created to be.**

*After Jesus' arrest the disciples fled—all but Peter and an unnamed companion. Instead of hiding, they followed behind the troop of soldiers that bore Jesus to the high priest's courtyard. Surrounded by soldiers and officials who hoped to see Jesus put to death, Peter's very life was at stake.*

*It isn't surprising, then, nor perhaps very cowardly, that when Peter was asked—not once but three times—whether he was one of Jesus' disciples, he denied it. The Gospels might not even have mentioned it except that . . . only hours before, Peter had twice declared to Jesus, "Even if I have to die with you, I will never disown you." [1]*

*Imagine facing Jesus again, knowing that you failed Him in His hour of greatest need. Would Jesus ever trust you again?*

---

Peter's mouth was dry. Dry from the salty swim, from excitement, from . . . shame. It was shame that knotted his stomach, twisted his tongue into silence. The instant he'd felt the tug of the great catch of fish in their nets, he'd known that the man on shore who'd urged them to cast their nets once more was Jesus. Without hesitation, he'd grabbed his cloak and dived into the water, the first to arrive at the feet of their Lord, their Savior.

*A hundred and fifty-three fish! As if we needed any gift other than the sight of Jesus, alive again,* he thought to himself. But now, sitting beside the fire, listening to James and John and Jesus, he wondered how Jesus could even bear to look at him. *Maybe He filled our nets as a way of telling me to go back to fishing. And to go back to my old name. Simon instead of Peter, the rock on which He was going to build His church. Instead, I was no better than Judas.*

In the days since Jesus' arrest, the scene in the courtyard had played over and over in Peter's thoughts and dreams. Asleep, shadowy guards seized him even as he shouted, "I don't know Him." By day, he tried to picture himself standing straight, saying to the servants in the courtyard, "Yes, He truly is the Messiah."

But he hadn't. He'd saved his own skin, saying not once but three times, "I'm not a disciple." *It's true, you aren't His disciple anymore. You let Him down, you who said that you were ready to go with Him to prison and to death.*[2] *How can you think yourself one bit better than Judas?*

He took a deep breath, trying to steady his pounding heart, then turned to stare dully at the familiar waters of the Sea of Galilee. The other disciples were talking earnestly with Jesus. He didn't dare look up for fear that Jesus would catch his eye. Better to let John and James do the talking. His own mouth had caused trouble for the last time.

He bit his lip. *Stop thinking,* he told himself. This afternoon he'd mend nets, keep his thoughts at bay.

A hand bearing fish and bread reached toward him. Jesus. Peter took the offering and mumbled his thanks. Then that most loved of voices whispered, "Simon, son of John, do you truly love me?"

Hot tears flooded Peter's eyes. "Yes, Lord," he answered hoarsely, "you know that I hope to count you as a friend." *Can I ask any more than to be a friend now? After I deserted him?* Peter looked down at the fish, crisp yet moist. Perfectly roasted over the fire. Jesus was serving *him* instead of the other way around.

"Feed my lambs," Jesus said softly. Peter lifted his eyes, expecting to see disappointment in Jesus' face. Instead, His brow was furrowed in concern.

"Simon, son of John, do you truly love me?" Jesus repeated as He knelt down beside the burly fisherman.

*He isn't sure,* Peter thought. *Why should He be?* Again looking down, he mumbled, "Yes, Lord, you know that I care about you." *How can I claim to love Him after I turned my back on Him?*

He felt Jesus take hold of his shoulders ever so gently, compelling him to look him right in the eye. "Then take care of my sheep. . . . Do you care for me?"

*He doesn't believe me,* Peter thought. *Then let me go away, leaving you with those you trust.* But then . . . Jesus' eyes crinkled ever so slightly, his mouth showing a hint of a smile. Peter took a deep breath and answered, "Lord, you know all these things; you know that I care for you." *I would follow you anywhere,* he wanted to add, but why would Jesus believe him?

"Feed my sheep," Jesus repeated, then let go of Peter and sat down, facing him. A full smile broke out on his Lord's face.

*"Feed my sheep. . . ."* Words that Jesus had spoken long ago came flooding back. *"My sheep listen to my voice; I know them, and they follow me."*[3] He was still inside the fold.

———————

*Jesus told His disciples that when a shepherd finds one lost sheep,* "he is happier about that one sheep than about the ninety-nine that did not wander off. In the same way your Father in heaven is not willing that any of these little ones should be lost."[4] *The following stories are from people who wandered. In each case, God helped them find the way home. That's what we can count on when we're searching for God; God is also looking for us.*

Cast all your anxiety on him because he cares for you.[5]

## A Time to Move On
*By Sharon Hinck*

The man in the chair across from me adjusted his glasses and picked up a note pad. "So it sounds like you're exhausted and you're being pecked to death by ducks."

I managed a hollow laugh. The counselor's description hit the target with painful precision. "But this is my lifework. I know God called me to this." I squeezed the bridge of my nose, feeling the prickle of tears. "It doesn't make sense. Why am I thinking about quitting?"

The man wrote a few notes. "Can you tell me more about feeling 'called'?"

I thought back to early steps on my vocational path and filled him in on the choices that had led me to this point. Over twenty years earlier, I'd attended a youth conference. The teacher of one breakout session demonstrated the use of dance in prayer and worship. Since my hunger for spiritual expression was followed closely by my passion for ballet and old musicals, I was entranced. The art of dance provided a way to express the deep feelings of worship that hummed inside me—a perfect combination of body, soul, and spirit.

I began to teach workshops with her at churches and conferences, and shared simple works of movement in worship services. Like poetry or paintings, dance gave people a new way of seeing. I loved the challenge of interpreting a hymn or Bible verse from a new perspective and wondered what more could be accomplished with dance as an expression of faith.

The specifics of my dream filled in slowly, like a pencil sketch dabbed with watercolors. After college I choreographed professionally in secular theatre. I longed to create theatre performances with trained artists, doing works that spoke to Christian themes.

In graduate school, another layer of color brought the picture into clearer focus. I met dance professionals who wanted to use their talents to express their faith in Christ. They longed to dance something besides *Swan Lake* or *West Side Story* but had no venue to perform works designed to celebrate God's love or reexamine familiar Bible stories.

An intense time of prayer, a network of artists, a generous and surprising financial gift from one of my dance students, and the completion of graduate school all opened the door to establish the company.

For years the dream blossomed. I dismissed as insignificant the long hours, financial struggle for our family, and physical exhaustion. We shared the message of God's love with folks who wouldn't step into a church, but were eager to attend a dance concert. Television interviews and performances expanded the reach of our ministry. I ignored the growing problems. Christians are supposed to press on.

After ten years, our patron support diminished. Needy artists sapped my nurturing instincts. Internal conflicts and external criticisms crushed me. I confronted the chilling thought of resigning as artistic director. But if I did, the board would close the company. Who else with my background would work for almost no salary? Closing the company could not be God's will, I insisted to myself.

But even my health conspired against me. Constant stomachaches and backaches drained the last of my energy. My whole body screamed for rest. Physical pain and emotional discouragement brought me to my knees—and to the three free counseling sessions that our insurance company provided.

I twisted a tissue in my hands and stared at the beige carpet in the counselor's office. "You don't understand. If I stop doing this, it means the last ten years were a journey in the wrong direction. All that effort wasted." My throat clogged and I pushed out the next words. "I failed God."

The counselor stopped scribbling notes and tapped his pencil against his chin. "I'll admit I don't fully understand the way you grapple with your spiritual life. But can I explore this with you?"

I nodded, even though I didn't think he'd have much to offer.

"Okay. You believe God called you to this work. For ten years you poured your heart into it. Signs pointed to a need to change direction, but you kept going until you had nothing left. Why would God want to torture you by putting a burden on you that you can't manage?"

I bristled. "That's the point. If I were better at trusting God, stronger in my faith, if I prayed harder . . . I should be able to keep going."

He frowned. "Describe God to me. Do you picture God as Father? Friend? Guiding Spirit?"

My lips twitched. "Drill sergeant. God's making me the best I can be." The pain and distortion of that image struck me even as I said the words.

The counselor nodded and waited.

I shifted in my chair. "I can't let this go. The ministry would die. I can't admit I failed."

"You shared from your heart for ten years. You followed God's call as you understood it. How is that a failure?"

"But I thought when I was eighty I'd still be choreographing . . . like Martha Graham did."

He smiled. "And maybe God has a different plan—in fact, maybe God's been trying to tell you that for the last several years."

The irony wasn't lost on me. Zen Buddhist books on his office shelves gave me a clue to his theology. I hadn't expected him to understand my faith crisis, yet he helped me see myself in a new way.

Was it true? Had I pressed on like a martyr while all along God was trying to get me to do something else? Was I working to please God when my Creator already loves me without reserve? How long had God been trying to get my attention?

As I drove home after the appointment, another hard question followed. Would I have the courage to follow God's nudging into a new direction—when I'd invested so much of my life in the dance company?

The transition hurt. The pain of stepping away from the ministry haunted me for years. My whole identity had been entwined in my work. In dark hours of insomnia, I asked "what if" questions and searched for ways I could have done better. Sometimes I felt despair at the things I'd left unfinished.

But other days, I leafed through files of letters from people who had attended a concert, or taken a dance class, or participated in a workshop. God reminded me that the ministry had fulfilled a purpose. One man wrote, "Your dance about temptation conveyed exactly how my battle with alcoholism feels to me. It really spoke to me. Thank you." A young ballet student colored a picture and scrawled, "Thank you for teaching me how to dance for Jesus." An older woman wrote, "I used the Lord's Prayer movements you taught with my prison ministry. The women at the jail were deeply touched by learning to pray in a new way."

Stepping out of one calling would have been much simpler if I'd immediately discovered a big, clear, new direction. Instead, God guided me into small assignments. Encouraging my husband, homeschooling my children, leading music for Sunday school, speaking at women's retreats, making new friends as I taught craft classes. Like tiles of a mosaic, my service now consisted of small pieces glued together in a pattern that I hoped made sense in God's plan.

One day I curled up on the couch, watching an old video of the dance company. My husband sank down beside me. "Do you miss it?"

I nodded. "Sometimes. I always knew exactly what I was supposed to be doing—and it felt great." I reached for his hand. "But I'm also relieved that God changed my direction. In a funny way I'm closer to God than when I was doing ministry full time. I'm less certain of my purpose but much more certain of God's love."

Our two youngest kids tumbled into the room and bounced onto the couch. "Let's go to the park."

I thought back to other times my children had called to me—harried days of rushing to performances, icing an injury, or waving them away as I made important phone calls. A precious segment of my life had been invested in the Christian dance company, answering a call to "move" for God. But my new calling led me into equally sacred places.

I turned off the video. "Yeah, we can go to the park. And grab some bread. We'll feed the ducks."

———

*In addition to the calling to nurture her family, God continued to move Sharon on into diverse adventures. However, her involvement in theatre, dance, music, and other arts focused on more manageable short-term projects. Her appreciation for God's love has deepened in the years since her difficult call to step away from what she had thought would be her "life work." In recent years she has focused on writing fiction and enjoys "choreographing" her characters as much as she used to enjoy setting dance works on her company. For more information on her recent projects, visit www.sharonhinck.com.*

## What Brought Us Together
*By Jane Kise*

Everything was ready for the bridal luncheon my mother was giving for me—chicken in the oven, broccoli steaming on the stove, the sherbet glasses chilled. We were just waiting for our last guest to arrive. My future mother-in-law gave me an apologetic glance and said, "Sandy should be here any minute. She was with her boyfriend this morning, patching things up, so she's driving separately."

"I'm glad they're speaking again," I said. Sandy was my fiancé, Brian's, sister, and I'd been around the family long enough to know that she and her boyfriend had a troubled relationship. If she was a little late, the rest of us would have more time to chat. After all, this lunch was a chance for my mom and friends to get to know my future in-laws.

Forty-five minutes later, we were still chatting, waiting for Sandy. My mother-in-law paced back and forth while my mother turned off the oven. We finally ate without Sandy, but the chicken was too dry to chew and the broccoli had turned to mush. She arrived almost two hours late, silent and sullen. I greeted her with a smile and hung up her coat, all the while thinking, *How could she let her personal problems ruin my luncheon?*

In those first months that I knew Sandy, I couldn't recall a single good time together. We had little in common, even though she was only a couple of years older than me. We didn't like the same movies, didn't read the same books or magazines. Still, I tried. I asked about her work and her friends whenever we were together. I remembered her birthday with a card and a call.

When Sandy married her first husband, Brian and I looked high and low for a unique gift, settling on a hand-painted pine chest that matched their bedroom set. We took the two of them to dinner and the theatre, but they arrived so late there was barely time to eat. *She's family,* I kept telling myself.

But we weren't friends. After holiday meals she darted from the table so fast that I assumed she preferred doing dishes to talking to me.

For my son's first birthday I shopped for party supplies at the store Sandy managed. "Why don't you make him a teddy bear cake?" she said. "I bet he'd love it!" It was the most enthusiasm I'd ever seen her show toward me. She filled my shopping cart with pastry bags, food dyes, candles, and a special bear-shaped pan. I must have looked worried, for she assured me, "I'll be there a few hours early to help you decorate it—I wouldn't miss my first nephew's first birthday!"

The morning of the party my mother-in-law called, saying, "Give my grandson a hug for me. Are you all set for the party?"

"I'm just waiting for Sandy to get here to decorate the cake."

"But, Jane, Sandy's here at the cabin. She came last night."

As I struggled to assemble the pastry bags, dye the frosting, and keep the birthday boy out of the way, I thought, *How could she forget?* I vowed never to count on Sandy for anything, ever again. I could be cordial; I could be polite. I could even be generous, but that was it. I wasn't going to risk having Sandy let me down.

For family gatherings I cooked things that I knew wouldn't dry out if she arrived late. For potluck dinners I asked her to bring salads or bread, things we could manage without if she didn't show up. Eventually she and her first husband divorced. A few years later, for her second marriage, all of us rallied around Sandy. Brian and I even supplied the wedding cake.

Still, as the years passed, I avoided her while keeping up a polite façade—one Christmas, I even spent hours making a calico goose similar to one she'd admired at a craft show. But we were not close.

Then one Labor Day weekend, the entire clan was supposed to gather at the family cabin. At the last minute everyone cancelled but Sandy's family and ours. All I could think of was the strain of being in that cabin for forty-eight hours with the one person in the world I couldn't get along with. How would I keep up the polite chatter?

The first day we kept busy unpacking and airing out the cabin. While our husbands headed the kids to the beach, Sandy and I exchanged polite greetings and marveled at how each other's children had grown.

"I brought some chicken and homemade cookies," I said as I unpacked our cooler.

"Good," she replied. "I've got hamburger and a cake. The guys can grill. How's your mom?"

"Fine. How's yours?"

Between lifeguarding our children and preparing dinner, the day passed quickly. After putting the kids to bed, I was relieved when Sandy switched on the TV. That way we didn't have to talk. A news bulletin flashed on the screen: Princess Diana had been gravely injured in a car accident.

Almost involuntarily I exclaimed, "No!" So did Sandy. "Surely she'll be okay," she whispered, looking stunned. "It seems like just yesterday that I was getting up at five A.M. to watch her wedding."

"I watched their fireworks celebration as I sewed the lace on my own wedding dress," I added. This latest news seemed like one more episode in Diana's never-ending drama, but we both went to sleep expecting that things would turn out all right.

The next morning our husbands headed out early to go fishing. The kids, exhausted from swimming all afternoon the day before, slept in. When I came into the kitchen, Sandy, eyes red, handed me the paper and said, "She died."

I stared at the headline in disbelief. The two of us were just slightly older than the princess.

Sandy and I poured ourselves a cup of coffee and sat down together at the kitchen table, the paper between us. I read aloud some quotes from a new biography about how the night before her wedding, Diana had felt trapped and uncertain of whether Charles could really love her.

Sandy interrupted me. "That's how I felt before I married my first husband. I postponed it twice because I was so unsure. I finally eloped with him so I couldn't back out of walking down the aisle."

The morning we heard that news was another I'd never forget. "I was so surprised that you actually married him."

Sandy looked puzzled. "Didn't all of you think he was perfect?"

"Well . . ." My eyes caught Diana's newspaper image, one that showed the longings behind the smile, then at Sandy. Her expression was a mirror of Diana's. I bit my lip. I'd easily empathized with the struggles and disappointments of a storybook princess I'd never met. Why hadn't I done the same for my sister-in-law? When, for all my pretense of being civil, had I ever really tried to get to know her?

As Sandy described how Diana's example had helped her start over after her divorce, my mind created a new list—a list of the ways I'd wronged Sandy. I'd been indifferent to her struggles. I'd frozen off any apologies she might have offered. Instead of forgiving her, I'd tallied up all the times she'd been inconsiderate. That morning I asked forgiveness for my years of coldness.

The barriers between us dissolved. With that, we began a conversation we should have begun sixteen years earlier, about her struggles with self-esteem. Chastened, I learned for the first time how fears of her boyfriend's reaction had kept her from leaving in time for that bridal luncheon so long ago. What did we have in common? In what remained of the weekend, we went running together, helped the kids fish off the dock, laughed ourselves sick trying to finish a crossword puzzle, and talked honestly.

That morning God not only showed me how wrong I could be about a person, but gave me a second chance—or maybe it was a thirtieth or fortieth or fiftieth chance—to become friends with Sandy. Today Sandy lives in a different state, but we keep up via e-mail with each other's families, successes, and frustrations. And we thank God that we finally drew closer together before she moved away.

---

*I sometimes wonder if I would ever have seen who Sandy really is if that picture of Diana hadn't come between us, but I also shudder at the thought of how many other ways God tried to tell me to start over with my sister-in-law. "Why do you look at the speck of sawdust in your brother's eye and pay no attention to the plank in your own eye?" [6] comes to mind, for example. Or, when Jesus told Peter to forgive his brother not just seven times, but seventy-seven times.[7]*

*God's will isn't hidden. Instead, in different ways and with various voices, God calls us back to what we were created to be, if only we are listening.*

## A Trusted Friend

*Walter Cone*
*As told to Evelyn D. Hamann*

My workday began, as usual, with a routine bus ride to downtown Tacoma. Though blind, I could feel the morning rays of the sun. We were due for a rather nice day in this usually wet season. Logan, my new seeing-eye dog of seven months, led me to a seat, then rested quietly at my feet. I reached down to scratch the top of his head. Logan and I were finally adjusting to each other, but at times I still longed for my old dog, Omni.

Omni was that one in a million for me; I wondered if I could fully trust another dog. After she retired, I'd gone through my share of replacements. One developed traffic-stress, making my commute almost impossible at times. Still another simply didn't get along with my wife. So much time, training, and emotional investment went into working with each dog that I was a bit discouraged.

I've been blind since birth, so you can imagine how much I rely on a dog. We work, walk, eat, and practically sleep together. To a dog, matching an individual's personality, stride, needs, and more isn't an overnight process.

Feeling a bit guilty for my thoughts, I reached down and gave Logan another scratch on the head. His brows rose expressively under my fingers as I gently stroked the short, soft hairs of his forehead. Our beginnings together had been eventful, to say the least.

Seven months earlier, I'd again returned to Guiding Eyes for the Blind in New York. Gene, Logan's trainer for the past year, brought him into the room where I waited. I reached down and tousled his sleek, short fur. He felt big and powerful, with strong leg muscles and jawline. Gene gave me his leash, saying, "Logan's a new breed of dog, a Brindle. He has the build and color of a black lab, with some of the markings of a Rottweiler. The light brown brows really make him look mischievous at times." I could hear the smile in Gene's voice. "He's a smart dog, and I believe you two are a great match."

My hope was short lived—Logan and I constantly battled wills for the next three weeks. I'd lead him up to an obstacle, give my command, and he consistently either dropped down and refused or did the opposite of what I asked.

Even so, along came our final exam: traveling unattended to a downtown store and retrieving a bag of chips. When Logan and I entered the shop, the smell of fresh fruit told me we were in the produce section. In an instant, Logan led me straight into a stack of fruit that toppled to the floor.

I apologized profusely to the gentleman in charge of produce and then directed Logan toward the middle aisles. I just wanted to get my assigned chips and get back to my room. I signaled Logan to round the corner, but he went straight. In the tug-of-war, he bumped me up against an end-aisle display. Every box seemed to fly from the shelf.

At least I couldn't see the stares directed at me and my dog. The manager called Guiding Eyes to rescue me *and* his store!

Later, Jan, the head trainer, came to visit me in my room. "Walt . . . well . . . despite what happened at the store, I think you are ready to go home."

"What?" I protested. "Jan, he doesn't even obey simple commands. There is *no* way we are ready to be on our own."

"You've got a very loyal dog, just what you need," she explained. "However, his loyalties are to Gene, his trainer. You need to get away from here so Logan can bond with you. Otherwise, his torn loyalty will continue to sabotage your working relationship. So have a nice trip home and good luck."

I was speechless. I reached down to give Logan's head a little scratch, but he turned away. I sighed heavily. *Lord, I just don't see how this is going to work.*

We headed home. Soon, our weeks together turned into months of daily harried bus trips and busy downtown traffic. Logan grew quite decisive on crowded sidewalks and crosswalks. He seemed trustworthy, just as Jan had predicted. And, like Omni, he got along famously with my family.

Still, I had doubts. Perhaps Logan was reliable for everyday situations, but Omni—she'd been rock-solid in adversity as well. How would Logan hold up in a high-stress situation? Would he spook, or develop permanent nervousness, making me have to start over again?

The bus suddenly came to a stop and the driver yelled out my destination, bringing my thoughts back to the present. I reached down and picked up my lead. "Okay, boy. This is where we get off."

I work in customer service at Lighthouse for the Blind. Many employees have disabilities of various kinds; several have working dogs. However, each day as we made our way through the first floor toward my third floor desk, Logan's presence drew multiple greetings from a group of workers who had both physical and mental handicaps. "Hey, Logan!" "There's *our* dog!" they'd say. Maybe it was the lilt of his brows or his strong build that caught their attention; I wasn't sure.

When we reached my desk, Logan immediately curled into his usual resting position by my foot. Between phone calls I reached down to give his forehead a scratch. "How ya doing there, boy?"

Suddenly a rumbling sound roared toward me. Everything around us started shaking. Earthquake, and quite a large one!

I slid off my chair and joined Logan beneath my desk, my heart pounding. All around the desk, ceiling tiles, computers, and other objects crashed to the floor. Dust and plaster filled my nostrils. I hugged Logan tighter, uncertain of what the next seconds would bring. There were at least two other seeing-eye dogs on the floor; one started to whimper. If that dog lost control, would Logan follow suit and leave me in the confusion?

I pulled him still closer. "How are you doing, boy?" His heartbeat seemed normal. Though alert, he seemed calm and sat firmly rooted. He nudged my cheek as if to say, "Fine, let's just wait till it's over." Even though the roof seemed about to fall down, Logan's unyielding steadfastness kept me calm.

It seemed an eternity, but things quieted down. Being blind, I couldn't assess the destruction or danger. "Logan, it's up to you, boy. What do you think?" Logan nudged me and rose, waiting for me to follow his lead. I could hear others in the confusion, running, some even crying, as they quickly exited. But Logan steadily led me forward, pausing and cueing me to turn right or left as needed. I never once stumbled over wires or debris. My heart pounded with excitement and pride as we stepped outside. I reached around my dog's neck, giving him a hug. "Good boy, Logan. You did well."

Someone near me said, "I don't know what to do. I can't find my workers. They must still be in there, but they won't let me back in the building."

I recognized the voice as one of the supervisors from the first floor; her workers were the ones who greeted Logan each day. From experience, I knew that mentally challenged individuals don't like broken routines, especially if something unexpected and stressful happens.

*I know that building better than most and I know right where to go,* I thought. *Logan sure seems ready to be the eyes for all.* I got down close to my partner. "Logan, are you up to it? Those people need us." I turned Logan around, gave the command, and away we went.

This time our assignment was a bit more important than retrieving a bag of chips. An eerie quiet surrounded each isolated noise that echoed through the mostly empty building. Logan led me around obstacles and down corridors. I couldn't tell if the halls were dark or well lit. Logan, though, seemed to know what to do and where to go. Finally I heard voices. "Hi, guys. Everyone here?" I shouted.

"Gotta work." "Got lots of work to do." I could hear distress in the workers' voices as they tried to bring order to the chaos.

"It's time to go. Can you follow me?"

"Nope. Gotta work."

I tried a different tactic. "Logan here says it's time to take a break."

"Logan?" came a small voice from one of the guys closer to me. "Hey, guys, Logan is here. He's our dog. He says it's time to take a break." More voices chimed in. "Oh, Logan." "Okay, time for break."

"Logan says he needs you to take hands and follow him out the door," I directed. "Are you ready?" I could hear and feel them as they gathered together and locked hands. We followed Logan's lead to safety and the warming rays of the late-February sun. I turned as I heard footsteps running in our direction. "Oh, Walt, you did it!" their supervisor shouted. "Hey, Walt got them out safely."

As hugs and reassurances were passed around, I lowered myself down. Logan was sitting beside me as calm as if he had just finished a nap, not a rescue mission. I ran my hand over those mischievous brows as his warm nose brushed my cheek. "Logan, you are a hero. It never would have been possible without you." Logan returned the sentiment with a warm lick.

I thought back over the past months, of weeks and weeks of safe bus trips, of journeys across busy streets too numerous to count, of the ease with which Logan had fit into our family. Why had it taken me so long to trust him when he was everything I needed all along? *God, let me be more open to seeing your hand on my life.* I guess you could say I definitely got my bag of chips!

———————

*Evelyn writes, "When I interviewed Walt for his story, Logan relaxed at his side. Though he basked playfully in the love my own children poured generously on him, I could see that his attention didn't wander far from his true master and friend, Walt. Three years later, Logan is still a trusted friend, continuing to lend his eyes to Walt."*

**KEY: No matter how or why you stumble, God stands ready to show you how to return to what you were created to be.**

Aren't we all like Walter Cone, looking for the perfect guide when the Perfect Guide is already leading us, each step of the way? God understands, though, just like Logan, and waits patiently for the moment when we step out in faith, ready to be led even in darkness.

"But what if I miss God's will? What happens then?" Perhaps you feel like you're not only in the dark, but on a tightrope, in danger of falling from God's favor into an abyss from which there is no escape. God's will isn't a tightrope, though. I once heard it described as more of a towrope.

Have you ever water-skied? The towrope is securely attached to the boat. Hang on and you can freely weave in and out of the wake, over waves and across the water. And if you let go, are you lost in the deep?

No, the boat circles back around and picks you up. You can start over, grasp the rope once more, and get up for another try.

So get ready to move. Consider Scripture, your design, circumstances, and any special messages you think God may be sending. Make your best, prayerful decision about what God wants you to do. Take that first step. Keep praying, keep watching, keep listening. And if you've strayed from God's path, rest assured that God will circle back around to help you head in the right direction.

> It's my choice
> Stay where I am,
>> knowing I'm not where you want me to be,
>> motionless, refusing to risk a misstep.
> Or step out,
>> hoping I'm headed toward the future you have in mind for me
>> yet unsure of the way.
> Only one choice draws me closer to you, Lord.
> You guide me in love, toward the center of your will,
>> whenever I look for you,
>>> listen for you, talk with you,
>>>> seek you without ceasing. Amen.

---

[1]Matthew 26:35
[2]Luke 22:33
[3]John 10:27
[4]Matthew 18:13–14
[5]1 Peter 5:7
[6]Matthew 7:3
[7]Matthew 18:21–22

# Going Deeper

# Bible Study and Reflection Questions

### Chapter 1: Why Is It So Hard to Discover God's Will?
*Key: The first step in finding and following God's will is giving our lives to God.*

1. The story of Lydia is found in Acts 16:11–15. Verse 14 says, "The Lord opened her heart to respond to Paul's message." According to the following verses, what keeps our hearts closed?

   - Psalm 138:6
   - Matthew 13:18–23
   - Luke 19:11–26
   - Colossians 2:8

2. By meeting regularly with other followers of Yahweh, Lydia was already searching for God. Why is fellowship important to us, according to these verses?

   - Matthew 18:19
   - 1 Corinthians 12:12–27
   - Hebrews 10:24–25

3. What do each of the following verses have to say about giving our lives to God?

   - Psalm 34:4–8
   - Psalm 84:10
   - John 14:23
   - James 4:8

4. Isaiah 48:17–18 tells us,

   I am the Lord your God, who teaches you what is best for you, who directs you in the way you should go. If only you had paid attention to my commands, your peace would have been like a river, your righteousness like the waves of the sea.

   What barriers keep you from trusting those promises from God?

5. In striving to give your life to God, as did the rodeo preacher and the foster parents in this chapter's stories, what is your biggest fear?

6. In Ephesians 1:17–19, Paul describes his prayers for the people of Ephesus. Use the following paraphrase of his words as your own prayer to draw closer to God.

> Lord, I ask for the Spirit of wisdom and revelation, so that I might know you better. Please keep my eyes focused and clear so that I can see exactly what you are calling me to do. Help me grasp the immensity of the glorious way of life you prepared for me. Amen.

7. Consider memorizing the words of Psalm 16:11 as an image of drawing closer to God:

> You have made known to me the path of life;
> you will fill me with joy in your presence,
> with eternal pleasures at your right hand.

## Chapter 2: What If I'm Just Not Sure What to Do?
### Key: God's will is about faith, not certainty.

1. Gideon's story is told in Judges 6. In verse 17, Gideon pleads, "If now I have found favor in your eyes, give me a sign that it is really you talking to me." Sometimes this text is used to suggest that we can ask for clear signs from God. Note, however, that Gideon was asking for guidance for a monumental task that would affect all of Israel. Consider what the following texts have to say about asking God for signs:

- Matthew 16:1–4
- John 20:29
- Hebrews 11:1
- 1 Peter 1:8–9

2. Read Hebrews 3:12–19. What does the rebellion of the Israelites in the desert, despite constant guidance, say about our faith?

3. Read Mark 9:17–24. What does this passage tell you about sharing your doubts with God?

4. In Exodus 3:12, God tells Moses, "I will be with you. And this will be the sign to you that it is I who have sent you: When you have brought the people out of Egypt, you will worship God on this mountain." What does this passage say about following God's guidance?

5. In our book *LifeDirections,* David Stark and I describe a life guided by God this way:

Realize that you've already won the race—that's the freedom we have in Christ and it's what allowed Paul to put his past behind him. That's the attitude with which we can approach finding God's will—we have the freedom to do our best. It's an adventure where we're guaranteed a safe ending, knowing that even if we somehow misstep, God will help us back on course.

How does this agree with or differ from your vision of a guided life?

6. What questions would you like to ask God about the stories you read in this chapter?

7. Consider memorizing the words of Psalm 143:8, 10 as a prayer for trusting the life God has in store for us.

> Let the morning bring me word of your unfailing love,
>> for I have put my trust in you.
> Show me the way I should go,
>> for to you I lift up my soul. . . .
> Teach me to do your will,
>> for you are my God;
>> may your good Spirit lead me on level ground.

## Chapter 3: What Can the Bible Tell Me Today?

### Key: The Bible is still our sovereign source for discovering God's will.

1. The story of the Council of Jerusalem is found in Acts 15. Both sides used Scripture to argue their beliefs about whether Gentiles should be circumcised. The fact that the Council settled the argument once and for all attests to the wisdom of their final decision.

   • Can you think of arguments within the church today where both sides use Scripture to support their views? How might we gain wisdom from the Council of Jerusalem?

   • Which of the following principles of using the Bible do you think the Church is weakest at today?

     • considering what the whole Bible has to say on a subject;

     • determining whether our question concerns a disputable or non-disputable matter (as discussed in Romans 14);

     • checking our interpretations with those of others in community.

2. What might God be saying about using the Bible for wisdom in the following verses?

- Psalm 119:33–40
- Psalm 119:89–104
- Proverbs 2:1–11
- Romans 14
- 2 Timothy 3:16–17
- James 1:22–25

3. Consider memorizing selected verses from Proverbs 2:1–11 (NRSV) as motivation to understand the Bible.

> If you accept my words
>     and treasure up my commandments within you . . .
> if you indeed cry out for insight, and raise your voice for understanding;
> if you seek it like silver,
>     and search for it as for hidden treasures—
> then you will . . . find the knowledge of God . . .
> Then you will understand righteousness and justice and equity, every good path;
> For wisdom will come into your heart . . .
> Understanding will guard you.

4. In the stories in this chapter, the Bible was used in very different ways. What questions do you have about how the Bible influenced their decisions or actions? Would you struggle to use the Bible in any of these ways? Why or why not?

   - In *Fear Not* Brenda recognized from the verses in Isaiah that God offered her a life without fear. She sought help from God to make that promise come alive in her life.
   - In *A Quarrel Not My Own* Jean used general principles in the Bible to guide her decision.
   - In *A New Relationship* Bible verses that caught Jill's eye convinced her that God was with her in the midst of her difficulties.

5. To use the Bible effectively, one needs to become familiar with the different ways it conveys God's wisdom—through history, stories, prophecies, poetry, letters to specific churches, and parables. The following steps make it easier for anyone to access its wisdom. Where do you think your knowledge of the Bible places you in this process? What might you do to move further along in being able to effectively seek guidance from the Bible?

   - Get to know the Bible before you need specific answers. Its core message is how God operates and seeks to establish a relationship with us.

- Find regular times or methods to read and study that suit you. Take a class, form a group, buy a study guide, listen to Scripture on tape—whatever appeals to you.
- Read the Bible in small pieces, giving yourself time to digest its messages.
- Learn to use tools for Bible study such as topical Bibles, concordances, chain references, and commentaries.

6. Examining what the whole Bible has to say on a topic takes practice. Use a Bible study tool to look at how the Bible's teaching changes on a specific topic, such as slavery, the role of women, the day we worship, or forgiving our neighbor.

7. Consider using Psalm 119:97–98, 103–104 as a prayer to encourage you to learn more deeply about the Bible:

Oh, how I love your law!
    I meditate on it all day long.
Your commands make me wiser than my enemies,
    for they are ever within me. . . .
How sweet are your words to my taste,
    sweeter than honey to my mouth!
I gain understanding from your precepts;
    therefore I hate every wrong path.

## Chapter 4: Can I Ever Trust My Own Heart?

### Key: The gifts and talents you've been given are part of God's plan for you.

1. Saul's story can be found in 1 Samuel 9–10. Why do you think Saul doubted that God had chosen him as king? Have you had experiences where people chose you for a task, yet you refused, thinking you didn't have the talents or gifts it required?

2. First Peter 4:10 (NRSV) tells us, "Like good stewards of the manifold grace of God, serve one another with whatever gift each of you has received." That means that *each of us* has gifts we can use. Can you list the gifts and talents that allow you to be enthusiastic, *en theos,* acting with God?

3. Some people struggle with a misperception that God didn't give them any important gifts. What insights can you gain from the following passages?

- Genesis 1:26–27
- Psalm 139:13–16
- Romans 12:6–8
- 1 Corinthians 4:9–11
- Ephesians 2:10

4. The three stories in this chapter suggest three ways God might guide us through how we were created. What questions do these stories raise for you?
   - Bill pursued his interests and passion for flying, despite obstacles.
   - Carol discovered that her talents, not just "open and closed doors," were guidance for what God wanted her to do.
   - Joanne saw a lifelong passion brought to fruition when she persevered.

5. How much of your time do you get to use your gifts? If it is less than sixty percent, is this temporary or chronic? What gifts might God be calling you to use now?

6. Because our passions can also overwhelm how God might otherwise be guiding us, through Scripture or our circumstances or other sources of wisdom, we need to test whether we're hearing God correctly. Consider the following:
   - Does the Bible prohibit my acting on this gift or passion?
   - Do others believe that God might be calling me to use my gifts this way?
   - Are my motives God-given or self-serving?
   - Do I and others feel closer to God when I act on my passion?

7. While your unique design is one of the ways in which God guides you, God can't guide you through this system until you like who you are. Consider using this paraphrase of Ephesians 3:18–20 as a prayer to help you reconsider what God might do through the gifts you were created with.

   Lord, help me grasp how wide and long and high and deep is your love, that I may know this love and be filled to the measure of your fullness. Help me believe that you are able to do immeasurably more than I can ask or imagine, by your power at work within me. Amen.

## Chapter 5: Was That God or Just a Dream?
   *Key: Test signs against Scripture and circumstances, yet trust that God may be drawing you closer.*

1. The story of Ananias is found in Acts 9:1–19. From this example, what might you conclude about how and when God guides us so directly?

2. The stories in this chapter give various forms of direct guidance, all similar to examples in the Bible. What questions do you have about being guided in these ways?

- Delores learned from a dream that God wanted her to take a missions trip.
- David followed God's direct command to go to a bookstore.
- Julie had a sign, the turkey, that God was with her. Her sister Beth had a vision that corrected how they were praying for their mother.

3. Consider what the following verses tell us about being guided directly by God.

- 1 Kings 19:11–13
- John 16:13
- John 14:16–17

4. Below are ways God led people directly in the Bible, with examples given. Have you, or do you know of someone, who has been led in these ways? Do you believe these still operate today?

- Dreams (Joseph, Matthew 1:18–21)
- People (David, 2 Samuel 12:1–8)
- Images (Jeremiah, Jeremiah 18:1–10)
- Prophecies (Simeon, Luke 2:25–35)
- Angels (Zechariah, Luke 1:5–25)
- Direct commands (Samuel, 1 Samuel 16:1–13)
- Visions (Peter, Acts 10:9–22)

5. In what ways are we vulnerable if we always look for this kind of guidance?

6. Have you asked for direct guidance and not received it? Why might God be asking you to rely on other forms of guidance, such as Scripture, how you were created, or what your situation can tell you about your decision?

7. Consider memorizing the following verses, John 14:15–18, as a source of wisdom in considering whether God might be guiding you directly.

   If you love me, you will obey what I command. And I will ask the Father, and he will give you another Counselor to be with you forever— the Spirit of truth. . . . You know him, for he lives with you and will be in you.

## Chapter 6: How Do I Know If Something Is a Sign From God?

*Key: God guides each one of us gently in ways we can best understand.*

1. The story of Paul's shipwreck on the shores of Malta is told in Acts 27:13–28:6. Why was the incident with the snake so significant to the islanders?

2. In each of the stories in this chapter, little, seemingly insignificant details convinced the writers that God was trying to get their attention. What questions would you like to ask the writers?

   • I took another look at dating after Brian suggested my favorite show and dinner.

   • Janelle felt affirmed to continue writing after seeing a yak, a yurt, a blue gnu, and Clifford.

   • Pam felt sure her mother's marriage was meant to be after finding purple bridesmaid dresses.

3. Use the words of Psalm 25 as a prayer to help you understand God's voice.

   Show me your ways, O Lord,
   　　teach me your paths;
   　　guide me in your truth and teach me,
   　　　　for you are God my Savior
   　　　　and my hope is in you all day long (4–5).

4. Consider how Jesus used objects and stories that were familiar to people to help them grasp complicated truths. As you look at the following examples, think of how they compare to the stories in this chapter.

   • Luke 5:1–7　　　　　　• John 4:1–26
   • John 1:44–49　　　　　• John 20:24–28

5. How do the words of Jesus in John 10:24–27 apply to understanding when God might be trying to tell you something through an everyday yet attention-grabbing event?

6. In his book *There Are No Accidents*, Richard Hopke[1] gives four features of synchronistic events that seem to have more than superficial meaning for our lives:

   • It's hard to see the cause/effect of relationships. For example, what

caused Brian to ask me out to *A Prairie Home Companion*?
- The event causes a deep emotional experience, as when Pam saw the purple dresses.
- The content of the experience is symbolic in nature, as with Janelle's yaks and yurts.
- The events almost always occur at points of important transitions in our lives, as were all of the stories in this chapter.

Compare Hopke's interpretation with the words of Psalm 139:1–16. Does God's intricate knowledge of our inmost being affect how we are guided?

7. As you work to interpret the events and stories of your life, consider the words of Paul in Philippians 4:8–9:

> Whatever is true, whatever is noble, whatever is right, whatever is pure, whatever is lovely, whatever is admirable—if anything is excellent or praiseworthy—think about such things. Whatever you have learned or received or heard from me, or seen in me—put it into practice. And the God of peace will be with you.

## Chapter 7: Doesn't God Open Doors?

*Key: Open doors don't necessarily point to God's will. Closed doors don't necessarily mean a certain path isn't God's will.*

1. Read David's story in 1 Samuel 24. Would you have interpreted David's circumstances as his men did or as David did? Why are we so quick to look for "open" and "closed" doors?

2. Read the following passages. What does Paul consider an open door?

   - Acts 14:19–28
   - 1 Corinthians 16:8–9
   - 2 Corinthians 2:12–13
   - Colossians 4:3

3. Below are a few Bible stories where those involved could have interpreted their circumstances as open doors or tightly closed doors. What insights can be gained from these passages?

   - Exodus 10:24–29
   - 1 Samuel 25:2–35
   - Mark 2:1–12
   - Acts 16:25–34

4. When have you interpreted circumstances as an open door (think back to Carol and the word processing job in Chapter 4), only to find out later that you had made a poor choice? What other method of

guidance (Scripture, your design, direct leadings) might have helped you choose more wisely?

5. In each of the stories of this chapter, the facts were only part of the message God was trying to convey.

- While Jeff's concerns about the health of the baby Pat wanted to adopt were legitimate (a closed door), God wanted Jeff to learn about turning over control.
- God wanted Dodie to step out in faith to help her daughter, not worry about the details.
- God wanted Deb to develop a new concept of home before going on with her life.

Think back on an incident where you had difficulty discerning whether circumstances were asking you to move forward. Did you learn something else as you worked through the decision?

6. Søren Kierkegaard wrote, "Life must be understood backward. But then one forgets the other clause—that it must be lived forward."[2] Think back on a decision that was filled with uncertainty. What did you learn as you struggled with your choices?

7. Consider memorizing the following verses as a reminder of the difficulty of interpreting our circumstances.

"For my thoughts are not your thoughts,
  neither are your ways my ways," declares the Lord.
"As the heavens are higher than the earth,
  so are my ways higher than your ways
  and my thoughts than your thoughts" (Isaiah 55:8–9).

## Chapter 8: What If I Don't Think I Can Do What God Is Asking?

*Key: The path before you may require the gifts of those around you.*

1. The story of Moses and Jethro is told in Exodus 18:13–27. When Jethro asks why people wait so long to see Moses, he answers, "Because the people come to see me to seek God's will" (v. 15). What does this say about Moses? About the Israelites?

2. Read the following passages. What principles can you glean for deciding whether or not a task requires the help of others?

- Genesis 2:18
- Ecclesiastes 4:9–12
- Mark 6:7–13
- Acts 6:1–7

3. Each of the stories in this chapter illustrated different traps of going it alone:
   - Evelyn and her sister-in-law, being overwhelmed by a false sense of duty;
   - Fred and his new office, not seeking out the talents of those he led;
   - Susan, thinking she had to "Mentor Mom" by herself or not at all.

   Which mistake might you be most likely to make?

4. Read the story of God calling Moses to go before Pharaoh in Exodus 3:1–12; 4:1–17. What can you learn from it regarding tasks that seem too big for you to handle?

5. In *LifeKeys*, we wrote, "Even if you are missing abilities that you believe are crucial, start to share your dreams with others, asking God to let them know if they are to join in . . . seek guidance as to how to carry on with it, whether or not you can do it alone."[3] What passion or ministry do you hesitate to act on, believing that you don't have all the necessary gifts? Have you shared the dream with others? What keeps you from exploring whether others would join you?

6. Romans 12:3–8 gives advice on assessing our gifts and putting them to use. Read the passage twice, paying special attention to the words, *think of yourself with sober judgment.* Do you tend to over- or underestimate how God has gifted you?

7. Use the following interpretation of Ecclesiastes 4:9–12 as a prayer for understanding how to join with others.

   Working together, we can increase the impact of our dream.
   If we fall, we can pull each other up.
   Alone, I can be overpowered.
   With another, we can keep going.
   Add a third and our dreams can endure.

## Chapter 9: If the Going Gets Tough, Did I Make a Wrong Turn?

*Key: Jesus' promise was twofold: "In this world you will have trouble. But take heart! I have overcome the world."*

1. The story of Barnabas and Paul's missionary journey is told in Acts 14. How do you think these experiences influenced their interpretation of "open" and "closed" doors?

2. Paul writes in Acts 20:23–24, "I only know that in every city the Holy Spirit warns me that prison and hardships are facing me. However, I consider my life worth nothing to me, if only I may finish the race and complete the task the Lord Jesus has given me—the task of testifying to the gospel of God's grace." How do his words differ from our modern-day view of hardships?

3. Read the following passages. What principles can be found in them for interpreting setbacks and tragedies in our lives?

   - Job 40:1–8
   - John 9:1–4
   - Philippians 1:12
   - Hebrews 12:1–2

4. In each of the stories included in this section, the writers could have interpreted their circumstances as evidence that God wasn't with them. Instead, as they opened themselves to God through journaling or prayer, they found that God was with them. Look at the following psalms and consider how they might provide similar assurance when you are caught in the world's troubles.

   - Psalm 3
   - Psalm 13
   - Psalm 22
   - Psalm 38
   - Psalm 91

5. Sometimes our circumstances *are* the result of poor choices we made, such as Samson's betrayal at the hands of Delilah, or the fallout from David's affair with Bathsheba. In many such Bible stories, God forgave the person's sins, yet the natural consequences still caused troubles in the person's life. Psalm 51 was written by David after the prophet Nathan confronted him about his adulterous affair. What can you learn about confession and forgiveness from David's words?

6. The full verse of John 16:33 reads,

   I have told you these things, so that in me you may have peace. In this world you will have trouble. But take heart! I have overcome the world.

   What might help you find the peace that Jesus offers, even in the midst of troubles? Ponder the psalms and the stories in this chapter for ideas.

7. Consider memorizing Romans 8:38–39 (NIV) as a reminder that God is with us, no matter what happens.

For I am convinced that neither death nor life,
> neither angels nor demons,
> neither the present nor the future,
> nor any powers,

neither height nor depth,
> nor anything else in all creation,
> will be able to separate us from
> the love of God

that is in Christ Jesus our Lord.

## Chapter 10: What If the Guiding Light Seems Dim?

*Key: God's guidance is more like a lamp unto our feet than a lighthouse beaming far into the future.*

1. The story of Joseph in Egypt is found in Genesis 37–45. Between the time his brothers sold him into slavery and the time they came to him for food, at least thirteen years passed. Only at the end could he say to his brothers, "You intended to harm me, but God intended it for good to accomplish what is now being done, the saving of many lives" (50:20). Ponder Joseph's story with regard to what it means for God's guidance as a lamp to our feet:

   - Lamps guide us through darkness.
   - Lamps give unsteady light.
   - With the dim light of a lamp, you might only see clearly enough to take the next step, not run ahead.
   - The darkness remains all around you.

2. Read Psalm 119:105–112, the section that starts with "Your word is a lamp to my feet." What insights do you gain from reading the whole passage?

3. What might the following verses have to say about moving ahead when you aren't sure where you're headed?

   - Proverbs 16:3
   - John 8:12
   - Isaiah 55:10–12
   - 1 John 1:5–7

4. In each of the stories in this chapter, the writers kept moving ahead, despite not understanding where the path was leading them. In each case, though, God somehow communicated the general directions to them.

   - Karen was convinced to write *Much Needed Bags* through dreams.

- Jane sensed God telling her to change the meeting time of her prayer group to create more ministry.
- I felt compelled through prayer to concentrate on our personal relationship and not our work partnership when Kelly confronted me.

What questions would you like to ask the writers of these stories or of God concerning how they were guided?

5. In Matthew 6:34, Jesus tells us, "Therefore do not worry about tomorrow, for tomorrow will worry about itself. Each day has enough trouble of its own." What does this verse say about moving ahead when you can't see where you're going?

6. In 2 Kings 5:1–15, Naaman, an army commander, asked to be cured of leprosy. Elisha the prophet sent a messenger to tell him, "Go, wash yourself seven times in the Jordan, and your flesh will be restored" (v. 10). Naaman refused, complaining, "I thought that he would surely come out to me and stand and call on the name of the Lord his God, wave his hand over the spot and cure me of my leprosy" (v. 11). Read verses 11–15 to find out what happened. How did Naaman decide to move ahead? What can we learn from Naaman?

7. Consider using Paul's words as a prayer to keep moving when the way is dark.

> I have learned to be content whatever the circumstances. I know what it is to be in need, and I know what it is to have plenty. I have learned the secret of being content in any and every situation, whether well fed or hungry, whether living in plenty or in want. I can do everything through him who gives me strength.[4]

## Chapter 11: How Can I Plan If My Future Is in God's Hands?

*Key: Living within God's will means looking for God, listening for God, talking with God, all without ceasing.*

1. Hannah's story is told in 1 Samuel 1. Her vow to God is given in verse 11, "O Lord Almighty, if you will only look upon your servant's misery and remember me, and not forget your servant but give her a son, then I will give him to the Lord for all the days of his life." Are there any ways in which her vow differs from bargaining with God? Why or why not?

2. What do the following Scripture verses have to say about planning, yet leaving things up to God?

- Proverbs 3:5–6
- Proverbs 14:22
- Proverbs 16:3, 9

- Isaiah 40:28–31
- James 4:13–16

3. In each of the stories in this chapter, the writers thought they had their futures figured out. Noel was not going to be a preacher's wife, Linda was going to be a mother, and Paul would continue as sheriff. What questions would you like to ask about how they let go of those plans? What lessons can you learn from their lives?

4. Ecclesiastes 3:1 tells us, "There is a time for everything, and a season for every activity under heaven." As you look for God's guidance, ask yourself what kind of season you're in.

   - A waiting place, not a final destination, like Joseph or Hannah?
   - A season where God is helping you explore different gifts or passions?
   - A season of healing, from sickness or hurt?
   - A season of parenting or caregiving that takes time?
   - A season where some of your circumstances can't be changed by your efforts?

   How might understanding the season you are in help you find God's guidance? How can we avoid using seasons of life as an excuse for ignoring God's leadings as to what we should do next?

5. Consider memorizing Jeremiah 29:11 as a source of hope in uncertainty.

   "For I know the plans I have for you," declares the Lord, "plans to prosper you and not to harm you, plans to give you hope and a future."

6. Scripture is full of stories where God provided clear guidance to people about their futures. Ponder the following stories and consider what they might have learned about God through their experiences. How did a glimpse of their futures help them? Hurt them?

   - God told Abraham that he would make his offspring like the dust of the earth, uncountable (Genesis 13:14–16). Years passed, yet Abraham and Sarah had no children. Abraham took matters into his own hands and had a child with his slave Hagar. Finally Isaac was born to Abraham and Sarah in their old age.

- Joseph dreamed that his brothers would all bow down to him. They grew so angry at his arrogance that they sold him into slavery (Genesis 37).
- God promised to bring the Israelites to "a land flowing with milk and honey" (Exodus 13:5), yet just a few weeks after their journey started, they grumbled, "If only we had died by the Lord's hand in Egypt! There we sat around pots of meat and ate all the food we wanted, but you have brought us out in to this desert to starve this entire assembly to death" (16:3).
- Saul anointed David king (1 Samuel 16:12–13), yet David's rule didn't begin for another decade.
- Jesus told Peter, "When you were younger you dressed yourself and went where you wanted; but when you are old you will stretch out your hands, and someone else will dress you and lead you where you do not want to go" (John 21:18), foretelling Peter's death.
- Paul told the leaders at Ephesus, "I only know that in every city the Holy Spirit warns me that prison and hardships are facing me" (Acts 20:23).

7. Use this paraphrase of Psalm 130 as a prayer for accepting that God's plan is best.

> I wait for the Lord, my soul waits,
> and in his word I put my hope.
> My soul waits for the Lord
> more than watchmen wait for the morning,
> more than watchmen wait for the morning.
> O Israel, put your hope in the Lord
> for with the Lord is unfailing love
> and with him is full redemption.[5]

## Chapter 12: What If I Missed God's Plan?

*Key: No matter how or why you stumble, God stands ready to show you how to return to what you were created to be.*

1. The story of how Jesus forgave Peter is told in John 21:1–23. Note that Peter denied knowing Jesus three times (John 18:15–27) and Jesus asked, "Do you love me?" three times. In the original Greek, Jesus asks if Peter loves him, using the word *agapaó*, which is the word for deep, divine love. Peter answers with the word *phileó*, the

word for being fond of someone. Peter, remembering his firm claim at the Last Supper that he would never desert Jesus, is now hesitant to proclaim the depth of his love for Jesus. Examine the story for the various ways Jesus worked to convince Peter that he was forgiven.

2. The three stories in this chapter tell of people who perhaps missed what God was trying to tell them. For Sharon, she ignored any hint that it was time to move on to a new ministry. For me, I'd missed that it was up to me to create a relationship. For Walt, he missed all the signs that he already had the right guide dog. What factors keep us from hearing God's voice?

3. The Bible is full of people who stumbled so badly that in our day they might not ever be trusted again. In each case, while forgiven, the person was still affected in some way by the bad choices they had made. What can we learn about God's plans for our lives from the following stories?

- Samson and Delilah (Judges 16)
- David and Bathsheba (2 Samuel 11–12)
- Zacchaeus (Luke 19:1–10)
- The woman of Samaria (John 4:1–42)

4. What do the following verses have to say about our ability to start over?

- Psalm 103:10–12
- Isaiah 1:18
- Micah 6:6–8
- John 8:1–8
- Romans 3:23–24
- Romans 8:28

5. When asked about their most vivid memory of a retiring pastor, one confirmation class cited a children's sermon where he had thrown a football from the front to the back of a sanctuary to illustrate Psalm 103:12:

As far as the east is from the west,
so far has [God] removed our transgressions from us.

What would help you visualize how completely God forgives us, "so great is his love for those who fear him" (v. 11)?

6. God leaves us free to go our own way. It's our choice whether we follow God's lead or not. Psalm 32:8–9 gives this advice:

I will instruct you and teach you in the way you should go; I will counsel you and watch over you. Do not be like the horse or the mule, which have no understanding but must be controlled by bit and bridle or they will not come to you.

What reasons have you found through these pages for making the effort to find and follow God's will?

7. Consider using this verse as your prayer as you work to find and follow God's will:

Commit your way to the Lord;
    trust in him and he will do this:
He will make your righteousness shine like the dawn,
    the justice of your cause like the noonday sun.[6]

---

[1]New York: Riverhead Books, 1997, p. 23.
[2]*Journals and Papers* (1843), vol. I.
[3]Kise, David Stark, and Sandra Krebs Hirsh. *LifeKeys: Discover Who You Are*. Minneapolis: Bethany House Publishers, 1996.
[4]Philippians 4:11–13
[5]Psalm 130:5–7
[6]Psalm 37:5–6

# Notes on Bible Sources

## Chapter 1

Lydia's story is found in Acts 16:11–15. The hymn the group sings is from Philippians 2:6–11. Paul mentions his "pedigree" as a Pharisee of the tribe of Benjamin in Philippians 3:5. As for Paul's little talk, in many of the sermonettes recorded in Acts, the apostles point out how the Jews didn't recognize Jesus as Messiah and use different biblical texts to show how He fulfilled the prophecies.

## Chapter 2

Gideon can be found hiding in the winepress in Judges 6. The chapter also describes how Gideon "put out a fleece" to be sure he'd understood God correctly.

## Chapter 3

The Council of Jerusalem is described in Acts 15. There are also references to it in Galatians 2, where Paul explains a bit of what took place behind the scenes.

## Chapter 4

The story of Saul's anointing as king is found in 1 Samuel 9–10. Saul's disobedience and loss of the Lord's favor is described in 1 Samuel 13:11–14.

## Chapter 5

Saul's persecution of the Christians in Jerusalem is described in Acts 8:1–3. Gamaliel's advice to the Sanhedrin is given in Acts 5:33–39. The story of Saul and Ananias is found in Acts 9:1–19.

## Chapter 6

The story of Paul and the people of Malta is found in Acts 27:13–28:6. I spent a summer in Malta, studying the legends and sites connected with the shipwreck of St. Paul. Two thousand years after those events, the islanders still are thankful that they learned about Jesus directly from one of the first apostles.

## Chapter 7

The story of Saul's persecution of David is found in 1 Samuel 24.

## Chapter 8

The story of Moses and Jethro is told in Exodus 18:13–27.

## Chapter 9

The story of Barnabas and Saul's missionary journey is told in Acts 14. In Acts 20:23–24, Paul described how the Holy Spirit warned him that hardships awaited him in every city, but those dangers were nothing "if only I may finish the race and complete the task the Lord Jesus has given me" (Acts 20:24). In Philippians 1:12 he echoes that the persecutions helped advance the Gospel.

## Chapter 10

The story of Joseph in Egypt and how he interpreted dreams is told in Genesis 37–45.

## Chapter 11

Hannah's story is told in 1 Samuel 1.

## Chapter 12

Peter's encounter with Jesus is told in John 21:1–23. His betrayal of Christ is taken from John 18:15–27 and Luke 22:54–62.

# Acknowledgments

## Chapter 1

"Cowboy Preacher Up" by David Kes, as told to Barbara Marshak. © 2004. Used by permission of the author.

"When God Opened Our Doors" by Gregg and Janet Anderson, as told to Jane Kise. © 2004.

## Chapter 2

"A Sister's Promise" by Harriette Peterson Koopman, as told to Connie Pettersen. © 2004. Used by permission of the author.

"How Can I Ask?" by Rhonda Jenson, as told to Jane Kise. © 2004.

"A Birthday Blessing" by Sheila McKinley. © 2004. Used by permission of the author.

## Chapter 3

"Fear Not!" by Brenda Henry. © 2004. Used by permission of the author.

"A Quarrel Not My Own" by Jean P. Swenson. © 2004. Used by permission of the author.

"A New Relationship" by Jill Samuelson-Omath, as told to Sharon Knudson. © 2004. Used by permission of the author. Sharon M. Knudson is a freelance writer and inspirational speaker. She serves as president of the Minnesota Christian Writers Guild (www.mnchristianwriters.org) and loves to teach writing classes. Sharon and her husband, Bob, are active in their church and live in St. Paul, Minnesota.

## Chapter 4

"Dreams of Flying" by Bill Yon, as told to Jane Kise. © 2004.

"Buried Treasure" by Carol Oyanagi. © 2004. Used by permission of the author.

"A Lifetime of Purpose" by Joanne M. Tarman. © 2004. Used by permission of the author.

## Chapter 5

"Mission to Mission" by Delores Topliff. © 2004. Used by permission of the author.

"Go!!!" by David Stark. © 2004. Used by permission of the author.

"God's Alarm Clock" by Julia Chapman (pseudonym) as told to Jane Kise. © 2004.

## Chapter 6

"A Neon Sign" by Janelle M. Huston. © 2004. Used by permission of the author.

"A Swirl of Purple" by Pamela Haskin. © 2004. Used by permission of the author.

## Chapter 7

"Who's in Charge?" by Jeff Dyson as told to Patricia Butler Dyson. © 2004. Used by permission of the author.

"My Heart Said *Go*" by Doris J. Davis. © 2004. Used by permission of the author.

"Finding My Way Home" by Deb Carriger. © 2004. Used by permission of the author.

## Chapter 8

"The Bath" by Evelyn D. Hamann. © 2004. Used by permission of the author.

"Listening" by Fred Scaife, as told to Jane Kise. © 2004.

"Tongue-Tied" by Susan Whitehead. © 2004. Used by permission of the author.

## Chapter 9

"*Not* on Our Own" by Barbara Marshak. © 2004. Used by permission of the author.

"Welcome to the Dawn" by Suzanne P. Campbell. © 2004. Used by permission of the author.

"Safe in God's Loving Arms" by Julia Nicole (pseudonym). © 2004. Used by permission of the author.

## Chapter 10

"Nehemiah Who?" by Karen J. Olson. © 2004. Used by permission of the author.

"A Quiet Promise" by Jane McClain. © 2004. Used by permission of the author.

## Chapter 11

"I Will Never" by Noel Piper. © 2004. Used by permission of the author.

"Counting the Cost" by Paul Tschida, as told to Sharon Sheppard. © 2004. Used by permission of the author.

"Setting My Plans Aside" by Linda Gilligan. © 2004. Used by permission of the author.

## Chapter 12

"A Time to Move On" by Sharon Hinck. © 2004. Used by permission of the author.

"A Trusted Friend" by Walter Cone as told to Evelyn Hamann. © 2004. Used by permission of the author.

Share your own story.

Read others' stories.

*click over to*

# www.findingandfollowing.org

*A Web site dedicated to collecting and featuring* **true stories** *of how God guides people.*